PRAISE FOR GOD-WIRED

As a person who can be very hard on myself because of the way I'm wired, but also impatient with others when they don't think like I do; God-Wired is a breath of fresh air. Chris Rollins and Ken Hartley help put together the puzzle pieces that bring all the uniqueness of individuals into a beautiful harmonious picture.

—Jason White, Senior Pastor, Gracepoint Church, Benton, Arkansas

God-Wired is the FIRST of its kind. It is a sensational, eye-opening, heart-felt and introspective literary masterpiece that combines faith and the marketplace together in a beautiful and tangible way. Ken and Chris have both spent decades in both the faith-based arena and the business arena and have co-created an absolute masterpiece that will help you to understand exactly how God created and wired you for Greatness! You will 10x your understanding of yourself, others, and God as a direct result of this book. Enjoy, apply what you learn, and share this book with others so that the planet can collectively SHIFT from Self-Wired to God-Wired!

—Dr. Delatorro L. McNeal, II MS, CSP

Peak Performance Expert & Global Keynote Speaker, Wall Street Journal & USA Today Bestselling Author of *Shift Into a Higher Gear: Better Your Best and Live Life to the Fullest*

I've heard DISC a lot. This is the first time I've understood it.

—Pastor Matt Smith, Refuge Church of the Assemblies of God, Jonesboro, Arkansas

Timely and on point. Not only do Ken & Chris bring to light how God uniquely designed each of us, they brilliantly lay out how effective communication goes way beyond the words we say.

—Gary Arblaster, Arblaster Consulting, Author of *Making Millions, Going Broke*

GOD-WIRED

You Are Uniquely & Wonderfully Made

Co-authored by:
Ken Hartley
Chris Rollins

ROLLINS
PERFORMANCE GROUP
PRESS

Published by Rollins Performance Group, Inc., Benton, AR
www.RollinsPerformanceGroup.com

Scriptures marked NKJV are taken from the NEW KING JAMES VERSION (NKJV): Scripture taken from the NEW KING JAMES VERSION®. Copyright © 1982 by Thomas Nelson, Inc. Used by permission. All rights reserved.

Scriptures marked KJV are taken from the KING JAMES VERSION (KJV): KING JAMES VERSION, public domain.

Scriptures marked NLT are taken from the HOLY BIBLE, NEW LIVING TRANSLATION (NLT): Scriptures taken from the HOLY BIBLE, NEW LIVING TRANSLATION, Copyright © 1996, 2004, 2007 by Tyndale House Foundation. Used by permission of Tyndale House Publishers, Inc., Carol Stream, Illinois 60188. All rights reserved. Used by permission.

This publication is designed to provide accurate and authoritative information with regard to the subject matter covered. It is sold with the understanding that the publisher and author are not engaged in rendering legal, accounting, psychological, or other professional advice. If legal advice or other expert assistance is required, the service of a competent professional should be sought. This book represents the collaborative ideas from Ken Hartley and Chris Rollins, which are derived from their collective years of ministry, biblical study, speaking, and training on human behavior.

Book Cover Design by Melissa Rollins

ISBN: 978-1-7338320-4-5 (Paperback)
ISBN: 978-1-7338320-5-2 (Hardcover)
ISBN: 978-1-7338320-6-9 (ePUB)
ISBN: 978-1-7338320-7-6 (Audio)

First Edition

CONTENTS

FOREWORD

I remember the first time I met Chris Rollins several years ago. His smile was contagious. Here was a guy who had never met a stranger in his life, who genuinely loved talking and interacting with everyone he met! He was real! My kind of guy! And Ken Hartley, another man with a great heart for people. He has more talent in his little finger than most people could develop in a lifetime! He is an entertainer, a TV personality, and a great educator. I call people like him "edutainers."

When I learned that the two of them were writing a book together, I felt my heart skip a beat! This is going to be good! And I have not been disappointed. They write in such a manner that the reader will think they are back in "story time" at school. Their methodology of telling a story is even better because the story has a point. They also accomplish this task as well. Tell a story, make a point. Make a point, tell a story! The greatest teacher who ever walked the face of this earth used that same teaching methodology because it communicates so well. It sticks in our minds.

Chris and Ken have masterfully created a way for you, the reader, to experience, at the same time, both personal growth and spiritual development. That is not an easy task to accomplish. Academic information alone is often "cut and dried." Spiritual knowledge is often heavenly minded but has no earthly good. However, with accurate educational information combined with stories, illustrations, and practical application, that is a sure winner every time! Congratulations guys . . . you did it!

I pray that this book has widespread distribution because people need hope and direction. I trust this book will bless the reader's life as it has mine and will help you see that you are fearfully and wonderfully made. When God made you, he did not make a mistake. He has a plan for your life, and understanding personality information is the surest way to find your path. When you understand personality information, as presented in this book, you see God's design in your life and the lives of the other people you know. It will give you the ability to see things that others often miss. In a word, you will be blessed.

Now read, enjoy, and be blessed!

Robert A. Rohm, Ph.D., President
Personality Insights, Inc.
Atlanta, GA

ACKNOWLEDGEMENTS

We both want to give a heartfelt note of gratitude to Dr. Robert Rohm. While a lot of organizations teach about personalities, communication types, and how those are impacted by the way each of us is uniquely wired, we both truly appreciate your heart-first approach to teaching the model of human behavior referred to as DISC, and how you are always looking to use it to find what is right with people rather than what is wrong.

Ken and I (Chris) met because of the passion each of us has for Jesus, leadership, personal development, and, of course, the DISC model of human behavior. We are thankful for John C. Maxwell, as without the connection we made through his leadership organization, this book would not exist today.

To you, the readers of this book, we sincerely hope that you will be encouraged as you read the pages that lie ahead. As you read the examples to come, we hope that you recognize your own personality expressed in some of the biblical and modern characters we discuss and that you see each of them in the positive way they are intended to be portrayed. As you recognize the ways in which you and others have been uniquely God-Wired, embrace the truth that you have an *amazing* personality style.

PREFACE

Deborah was one of the most beautiful women any man had ever seen. At least, she used to be. But that persona was now buried under years and years of abuse. All that was left on the surface were wrinkles and scars, the byproducts of an extraordinarily rough life.

Deborah's father had died when she was very young. Her mother did the best she could, but the stress of providing for two children proved too much for her heart to bear, and she also died. The culture in which Deborah lived was not kind to women. Her little brother was taken as an apprentice to a carpenter. The carpenter's wife made rugs. She tried to get the wife to teach her that trade, but it seemed the family's only interest was in helping her brother. She was satisfied knowing he would be taken care of, even though she never saw him again after they parted ways.

Deborah had no means to provide for herself, so she began to beg in the streets. Her only means of provision was the generosity of others, and that was running thin. She needed money to buy necessities, but if she was honest with herself, it was the communication with another human being she was missing. In a short time, she had exhausted every other avenue of acquiring money, except for one.

Many men near the city entrance commented on her physical beauty. She noticed some of the same men walking by her multiple times a day. Some made lewd comments when no one else was listening. She tried to ignore them.

There was another woman at the city gate who was much older than Deborah, and she noticed how men also talked to her. She wasn't sure what the other woman did for a living, but she could guess. The other woman noticed that she had no place to go at night and invited her to stay with her. What choice did she have but to agree? Where else could she go? All of her relationships on the earth were severed.

The woman's name was Abigail. Her house was decorated immaculately. She talked to Deborah about a different way to make a living. She looked her in the eyes and explained how she could easily adapt to this lifestyle. She seemed to care about her. All it took was a few minutes of courage, and she would be able to provide for herself in ways she had never dreamed of before. It had been so long since Deborah had really talked to anybody that her heart told her this was the right pathway for the time being.

Deborah knew exactly what she was getting into, but again— what other choice did she have? The next time she was at the city gate, she was no longer begging. Abigail had dressed her very differently and told her a few things to say. In a very short amount of time, a man approached her, and they communicated very differently than they had before. A business transaction was made, and off they went to Abigail's house to Deborah's room.

The first time, it cost her innocence. The second time, it cost her emotions. After the third time, it cost her mental stability. After the fourth time, it cost her soul. She became a shadow of who she was. From this point on, everything she did was the same thing, with no substance behind it. She went through feeling shame, anger, hatred, self-loathing, and eventually detachment from all emotions as a result of the faceless men who used and abused her. The emotion of the event was completely separated from her. Men were nothing more than goats to be milked of their resources and thrown back into the herd, which is what she did, time after time.

Abigail eventually left, and Deborah continued on by herself. Months turned into years. Nothing mattered. Every day was the same abuse with a few of the same faces, but mostly different ones.

So, when the religious authorities burst into her house, the man jumped out the window and fled. But the authorities never even pursued him. They just grabbed her, half dressed, and dragged her into the street in front of a large crowd, gathered to watch the commotion, and threw her at the feet of a man she'd never seen before.

The accusation was shouted by the Pharisee, "Teacher! This woman was caught in the *very act* of adultery. The law of Moses commands us to stone such a woman. But what do *you* say?"

The Pharisees stooped, and each one picked up a large stone in their hands, ready to act. Deborah knew the consequences, but she was confused. Some of the men who had dragged her into the street were clients of hers. They had never bothered her before. Why now?

She didn't dare look at them, but at one point, her gaze slowly raised to the man in front of her—the man being questioned by the Pharisees. He was looking at her, and for a brief moment, their eyes locked. She'd seen hundreds of men—all the same, but not this one. This man was different. Something in his eyes showed truth, love, and compassion that she had never known.

What seemed like minutes of silence spent gazing at each other was actually a couple of seconds, and she closed her eyes and looked back down in time to see a tear fall into the dirt below her. Then, as she gazed ahead, she noticed the man began to use his finger to write in the dirt. It was directly in front of her. She couldn't help but see it. She began to make out the names of some of the religious authorities who were her clients. Somehow, this man knew! But how?

Then she heard him speak for the first time, with strength and authority, to this religious group: "Let you who are without sin cast the first stone." There was an audible gasp in the crowd. The Pharisees looked in disbelief at the names in the dirt. One by one, they dropped their stones and walked away.

And then she heard something she never expected: "Woman?"

The man addressed her directly. Oh, she had been addressed by men before, but not like this. Normally, a man only addressed a strange woman in this culture for one reason, which she knew all too well. She had been solicited by men before, but this was different. There was compassion in this man's voice. He showed her mercy. This man was giving, not taking.

He asked, "Where are your accusers?"

With extreme hesitation, she looked around and saw no one, then replied, "They are gone."

A slight smile crossed his face as he continued, "Then neither do I condemn you."

She felt a weight lifted from her and a freedom rush into what she thought was a previously dead soul. Years of abuse began to melt away. There was a sudden awareness of her lack of dress as she covered as much of herself as she could. What could she possibly do in return for what this man had given her?

Before she could say anything, he looked her in the eyes and said, "Go. And sin no more."

And from that day on, she didn't. She was a different person because of the way this man connected with her. This man who saw something in her she no longer knew was there. From that day on, everything changed for Deborah.

For most of her life, people had communicated with her in various ways. But this time, for the first time in her life, someone went beyond communication with Deborah. He actually _connected_ with her.

And it changed her life.

PART I

Laying the Foundation

INTRODUCTION

WE SEE IT EVERY DAY!

A "Typical" Corporate Meeting

The sunbeams shone through the blinds onto the cherry conference table of the Exeter Corporation. The brown leather chairs stood in contrast to the expensive, blue Persian rug on the floor beneath the table.

Sitting around the table were Isabel Bright, Sam Humble, Daniel Lyon, and Carissa Cooper. Isabel was talking away to Sam, who seemed genuinely interested in what she was saying. Carissa organized notes in front of her, skimming through them while making a few extra notations. Daniel had his face buried in his phone, checking the latest status of the stock market. The door flying opened caused him to throw the phone down and look up.

Jamison Smith, the president of Exeter, powered through the door, causing everyone to snap to and move their attention to the head of the table. With a large portrait of himself centered behind him, he boomed, "Okay, everybody. We've been talking about getting the new campaign finished for the Exeter product launch. We've talked and talked, but today I want results. That means before any of you leave this room today, I need answers and a definitive plan. Get it done."

And with a turn on his heel and a slam of a door, he was gone, leaving the group speechless for ten awkward seconds, which was longer than the meeting that had just happened.

Isabel's thoughts ran across her face, and although she didn't say it out loud—which was unusual for her—most anyone could have read her expression from anywhere in the room: *Wow. That was so intense. He has such passion! He just needs to learn to have some fun every now and then. I wonder if he'd go to an escape room with all of us.*

Sam's thoughts were his own but just as real: *He is one of the most demanding, rude dictators I've ever known. He just comes in, barks out orders, dumps everything in our laps, and then expects us to fix it so he can look good. What a jerk!*

Daniel spoke up, "Okay. Let's get on this. I have important things to do."

Sam thought, *He and Jamison are just alike. They act like they're the only important ones here. I'm sure neither of them even know what the rest of us do to make things happen. It's obvious that they don't care either. I doubt they know that my sister is in the hospital. They never bother to ask about anything other than what they want. If insensitivity was a currency, they'd both be billionaires.*

Daniel continued, "Let's agree on the plan I presented at the last meeting. It's simple, and it'll work."

Carissa normally didn't speak up unless she was asked questions, but she couldn't keep quiet on this one, countering, "Except that your plan will put us over the budget by thirty-four percent, and that will not be acceptable. We must stay within the boundaries we've been given."

Daniel shot back, "Look! I get it. It costs more. But the old man can't have everything he wants. If he wants it this quickly, we're going to have to spend more. I learned a long time ago that you can't have it your way every time. Life just doesn't work that way."

I wonder if you even realize the words coming out of your own mouth, Sam thought. *You have to have your own way in every conversation. Nobody gets a word in edgewise as long as you're in the room.*

Isabel chimed in with a bubbly tone, "Why don't we make this a game? Every person can share an idea, but whatever letter the last word they use starts with, the next person has to start with that letter? Yes? Doesn't that sound fun?"

Everyone stared for a moment.

Daniel, ignoring her, continued, "Moving on. Let's put my idea back on the table. I think we should all vote on it so we can get out of here and get back to being productive in our own offices."

Carissa just looked at Daniel, this time without saying a word and thought, *I'll speak to finance about this later today. This can't go on like this.*

Daniel continued taking over the meeting: "Here. Here's the proposal. I'm saving you time. Let's all sign off on this and get going."

Isabel reached out first and signed at the bottom of the document. "I'll sign this. I really like you, Daniel, and you have good ideas. But can we all at least go eat together and talk? We all need to catch up!"

Daniel slid the folder over in front of Sam, who quietly signed his name, along with a forced smile.

The proposal finally made its way to the final signature, Carissa. She looked down at the paper, then stared straight ahead and flatly said, "I'm not signing that."

Daniel almost exploded, "Why not? It's a quick and easy solution, and you know it."

Carissa calmly responded, "No. I don't know that. It may be quick and easy, but I don't believe it's the right solution."

Daniel replied condescendingly, "Yeah, you always know the right solution."

Isabel jumped in at light speed: "Well, to be honest, she does know a lot of procedures and policies. She can quote them. She's told me several of them before—"

Daniel interrupted, "I know. She's told all of us. It's like she's our mother."

Isabel continued sympathetically, "Well, I think that's sweet. This world could use more mothers. Mothers are kind and special and caring and loving. Plus, they're a lot of fun. They feed you well, and they know how to talk to you about—"

Daniel interrupted again, "I already have a mother. And she's not it."

Sam's eyebrows raised as he thought, *Wow! He does have a mother. Who knew?*

Carissa replied with no emotion behind her delivery, "I am not trying to be anybody's mother. But I'm pretty sure none of us want to have to answer to Mr. Smith about being over budget. Also, section three of your proposal is dangerously close to noncompliance and could get all of us into trouble."

Sam cleared his throat.

Everyone stared, waiting for him to talk.

Clearing his throat again and stammering, he eked out, "Sorry. Allergies."

"If you have something to say, Sam, go ahead," Daniel said in a challenging tone.

Carissa encouraged, "Yes, Sam. We're all open to everyone's opinions and perspectives. Please—go ahead."

Isabel practically exploded, "Yes, Sam. You're so wonderful! Everyone here loves you. How could they not? You're so sweet and encouraging to everyone. You're thoughtful. You give us those wonderful cards on our birthdays. Besides, you're fun! So go ahead! Talk. Tell us what you think! Go ahead. Please! Come on."

Daniel rolled his eyes. "Maybe he will talk if you'll finally shut your mouth."

Isabel looked shocked. "Well, that was uncalled for."

Carissa encouraged again, "Please, Sam. Tell us what you think."

Sam took a deep breath, then stuttered, "Okay. What I think. Well, uh, I think . . . I think . . ." He cleared his throat again and then spoke with more deliberation. "I think it's not useful for us to bicker. Sharing differing opinions is important, but arguing over who is right is not. I don't know about anybody else here, but that type of interaction stresses me out. Why can't we all just get along and focus on our strengths?

"Daniel, you're great as a visionary, but let's be honest, Carissa is better at taking care of details. You don't like details anyway. Isabel is better at connecting with people than any of us. Why doesn't everyone just run in their strength zones so we can succeed together? In my mind, doing this together is the best way to get it done."

And after a pause, he sincerely asked, "Can we please just work together?"

Isabel teared up and said, "Oh my gosh. That was beautiful. I just love that."

Carissa, still unemotional, thought for a moment, then said, "I'm willing to do that if everyone else is. I think Sam's suggestion would be the most efficient and effective way to get this done."

Daniel looked at Carissa then said, "So you're going to do all the legal and financial tweaks needed to make this work?"

Carissa replied, "Absolutely. I'll do my best. And I'll show it all to you so you can all approve it, and Daniel, if you like, you can make the presentation on behalf of all of us to Mr. Smith."

Daniel thought for a moment, shrugged his shoulders, then said, "Agreed."

Isabel cheered. Sam smiled. Carissa opened the paperwork, took out her red pen, and silently but diligently went to work.

Daniel asked, "So are we meeting back here after you're done, Carissa?"

Isabel pounced, "Oh no! Remember? Mr. Smith said we have to stay here. I'll Door Dash our lunch, and we can go around the table and talk about our families and even our dreams! It'll be awesome! Like the best lunch EVER!"

Daniel stared blankly, then picked up his phone and started texting. Sam smiled at Isabel then said, "I'll eat, but beyond that, that's all I'll promise."

A Typical Church Committee Meeting

Cars sped by on the busy, six-lane thoroughfare in front of the strip mall where Celebration Church was located. The church had purchased the property after ShopMart moved closer to the interstate three years ago. They did extensive updates inside to give it a welcoming lobby area, where people could visit and have the trendiest coffee. The auditorium had about 800 chairs set up in front of a raised stage that was only accessible through the doors on either side. A large LED wall featured a repeating, colorful pattern while worship music played in the background.

On the stage, on this Saturday morning, were four folding chairs in a semicircle and one chair sitting in front of those. Pastor Loren Hamilton had planted the church and led it as the senior pastor for the last four years. In the chairs sat the volunteer leadership of the church, and they were all excited to be hiring a brand-new, full-time staff member to lead the youth and children's ministries (or "Next Gen Pastor," as they would be known).

Their search had led them through twenty-five resumes, and during that process, they had now narrowed the choices down to two people: Thomas and Jody.

Sitting in the chairs were Desiree Dawson, Isaac Giles, Sharon Thomas, and Christopher McNeal. Each volunteer brought unique perspectives to the group, and Pastor Loren knew it. He was known as a sensitive and caring pastor, who knew the names of every family that attended Celebration Church. He was active in serving in the community food bank and on the committee to provide assistance to the homeless. His messages on Sunday morning were heartfelt, and he was able to pull deeper truths out of the word of God, and yet, make them accessible for anybody to grasp. He was also one of the best "people-persons" anyone could possibly know. He had an innate sense of people's personalities and drives, so when he chose this committee to help find their Next Gen Pastor, he selected as eclectic and diverse of a group of people as possible.

"Okay, folks. First of all, thank you for all of your service. I know I've said that to you several times in this process, but I cannot thank you enough. You're all very special to me, and I realize you're all volunteers with busy careers of your own. Saturdays are precious times for busy people like you, and I want to be respectful of that time."

He was exactly right. Desiree worked at ValTech, one of the largest technology development companies in the world. She had started at an entry-level job there fifteen years ago, and she systematically worked her way to the top through her work ethic and reputation for success at whatever she put her hand to as well as her high-powered, driven personality. She was now the CEO of ValTech and highly respected in the community and the church for her leadership and influence.

Isaac Giles worked at an advertising firm in town. Many national brands sought out the firm for the clever, creative, and fun ways they made their brands unforgettable. And behind most of those campaigns was Isaac. In fact, Isaac conceived and developed the entire branding and decoration of the children's wing of Celebration Church, and other churches often visited it as the new standard for children's departments at churches. Isaac was also a stage personality when the church needed to add an element of excitement and fun to announcements, but he especially shined on stage during their holiday programs, often landing the lead role and having everyone in the audience in stitches.

Sharon Thomas worked at the hospital in the administration wing since she'd graduated from college twenty-five years ago. A quiet, shy person, she worked in the accounting department. She always completed her work with excellence, received numerous awards, and was offered several promotions during her tenure, but she politely turned down each promotion, saying, "I love what I do and have no desire to do anything else." Even though she wasn't out in front, everyone at the hospital knew she was the backbone of the department that made everything run smoothly.

Christopher McNeal worked as the human resources manager for Jordan Financial, a large investment firm on the twenty-eighth floor of the tallest building in the downtown business district. He was known to be fair but tough in his dealings. He had a very no-nonsense approach to his job and drew very clear lines about what was right and wrong, never deviating from those boundaries.

Pastor Loren knew the differences of each person, but he also knew the value of diversity of opinions, often quoting the "iron sharpens iron" Scripture as to his reasoning for putting a group like this together.

He continued, "We need to make an offer to either Thomas or Jody, but that choice is going to be yours, not mine."

Desiree asked, "Which one do you prefer, Pastor?"

Loren smiled back. "I like them both." This comment brought eye rolls from both Desiree and Christopher. Loren saw both reactions and responded, "Seriously. I like them both. You've all done a stellar job narrowing this down to two highly qualified and wonderful candidates, and I could easily work with either one. The final decision is going to be yours. The Bible says there is wisdom in a multitude of counselors, and I consider you all to be very wise and I trust your judgment. I'm going to my office, and I look forward to hearing what you decide." And with that, he stood up, smiled, and calmly walked off the stage.

Once the stage door shut behind him, Desiree took charge. "I know we all have opinions. We've all been listening to these two exclusively for more than a week now, but in my mind, Jody is the clear choice. He has a proven track record of building a solid youth group in his current church. He has been in ministry full time for eight years and understands the work expectations and," pausing for emphasis, she continued, "he's organized."

Then, turning in a somewhat dramatic but strategic way to Christopher, she asked, "What do you think?"

Christopher reached into a bag next to him, pulled out four copies of a small folder, and began handing each person a copy. "I've completed a side-by-side comparison of Jody and Thomas for everyone to see, showing their education, experience, as well as the numerical growth of their respective ministries. I've also included the DISC assessment, Enneagram, and Myers-Briggs results for them. I typed out both of their personal testimonies they gave us from their respective Zoom interviews for everyone to read. Based on the statistics I'm seeing, I tend to agree with Desiree that Jody is our best choice. He has more experience. The numbers tell me he knows what he's doing; plus, he is very organized."

Sharon replied to the last comment, "And maybe a little robotic."

Desiree seemed surprised at this, questioning, "Robotic?"

"Yes. Robotic," Sharon explained. "These reports don't tell us the entire story."

Christopher countered, "Their testimonies are here."

Sharon went further: "These are numbers and statistics, but let's be real here. This is about relationships. Youth aren't going to come to our church because we show them statistics. They come to church because of the relationships and connections they have with their friends and with this person. If the kids don't connect with their leaders on a relational level, we won't keep them. They'll just go where they have those connections. Thomas connects."

Desiree asked, "Are you sure that's not just because his first name is also your last name?"

Sharon sighed. "That has nothing to do with it. It was that he was warm and caring. He was much more like Pastor Loren. He took the time to talk with the kids. He had more to do with them off the stage than he did simply speaking to them from the stage. That's important, and it isn't a statistic you can qualify on a piece of paper."

Isaac spoke up: "I agree with Sharon. I liked Thomas. He has a great personality. I mean, we connected immediately. He saw my *Star Wars* T-shirt and started asking me about it. He knew all about the *Mandalorian* episodes, and we talked about the most recent movies versus the classic ones. Some of the students gathered around us and joined in. Yeah. Thomas is great. I like him a lot. He's fun. He's energetic. He's relational. His stories were funny. He cared about the students. It was all heart with him. You just naturally love the guy."

Desiree chimed in a bit sarcastically, "And he likes *Star Wars*."

Isaac answered, "Oh, come on, Desiree. It's not just that."

Christopher jumped in, "Statistically speaking, *Star Wars* hasn't been as big since George Lucas sold it."

Isaac shot back, "That's not true. The last three films grossed over a billion dollars."

Christopher countered, "That's only because the ticket prices are higher. The audiences have dropped. And the newer films have been widely criticized compared to the originals. I can show you the article that has all the stats in it to prove I'm right on this one."

Isaac answered, "I have no doubt you can. I'm good. But we can all agree that the classics are way better than the new ones, right?"

Christopher and Sharon agreed, "Yes!" Then they started talking about things they liked in the original trilogy.

Desiree didn't say anything but then finally admitted, "I am happy to say I've never seen one of those films." They all stopped talking at the same time and simultaneously looked at her.

Sharon's eyebrows raised. "Really? Never?"

Desiree shook her head. "Nope. I don't waste my time on things like that."

Christopher seemed amazed. "Wow! You do realize that puts you into a unique demographic, right?"

Isaac muttered, "I'm actually not surprised at that comment. I totally cannot see you in a movie theater watching a movie, much less anything relating to *Star Wars*."

"Ah. Excuse me," someone interrupted. It was Pastor Loren.

Reaching down to the chair he previously occupied, he picked up his cell phone. "Sorry. I forgot this. But before I leave, I *must* know how we got from choosing our Next Generation Pastor to a debate about *Star Wars*."

Desiree and Christopher simultaneously pointed at Isaac. Christopher then answered, "They're proposing we vote for Thomas based on the *Star Wars* connection, but I'm trying to bring them to the dark side to vote for 'Jody Wan Kenobi.'"

Isaac seemed a little shocked and half-laughingly replied, "Wow, Chris! A joke! And a decent one at that."

Desiree pounced, "Chris? You know he prefers Christopher."

Isaac immediately replied, "I'm sorry. I didn't mean anything by it, Christopher. My bad, Desi."

Desiree raised her eyebrows at him like a parent about to scold a child. But before she could say anything, Isaac raised his hands in a surrendering motion and said, "I'm just joking! My name does mean 'laughter,' you know."

"I know. Your parents named you appropriately for sure," Christopher replied with a smile.

Sharon seemed to be a little upset. "I have to say. I shared my heart with all of you about how I felt, and you all seemed to ignore it. You turned this into a completely different conversation. Jody is great. He's a powerful, engaging speaker and brings a lot of organizational skills to the table, but I want our youth to have a loving pastor—just like Pastor Loren."

Loren replied with a kind smile, "I truly appreciate that, Sharon. You all have different, but great perspectives you bring to the table, which is why I asked you to serve on this team. Desiree, you asked me how I felt about Thomas and Jody. After thinking about it for a moment, I do feel like I need to interject one thing: Thomas and I connected from the standpoint that we are a great deal alike. We tend to process things similarly. But I want us all to consider the advantages of having someone here not like me too. Just like this diverse group brings something incredible to the table, consider that having a diverse leadership team could do the same thing. Think about it."

After Pastor Loren exited again, the team talk went in a new direction with a new perspective. After a ten-minute discussion, they unanimously agreed to bring Jody in as the Next Generation Pastor. They all knew a Discipleship Pastor position was on the horizon in the next six to twelve months, though, and they all agreed Thomas would be ideal for that position.

Who Was Right . . . and who Was Wrong?

While both stories were fictitious to protect the innocent (or maybe the guilty), you probably read at least one of those examples and immediately thought of a memory from your own experience that sounded very similar to what you read. It is very likely that you quickly related with one or two of the people in the meeting, while possibly identifying a person or two who represented those who are always causing problems in meetings. Why do you think that is?

The interesting thing about each scenario is that our goal was not to demonstrate who was "right" or "wrong." The "You must be wrong in order for me to be right" mindset is often one of the greatest causes of miscommunication. It truly comes down to the unique perspective that each person can bring to a situation. Only when every potential point is considered can you see the full picture of the challenge in front of you. To miss any possible perspective causes us all to have blind spots, which can ultimately hurt our ability to make the best decisions possible.

It's a nine!   It's a six!

1

ONE BODY, DIFFERENT PARTS

The art of communication is the language of leadership.

—James Humes

One of the funniest movies ever made, in my (Ken's) opinion, is *What About Bob?*, where a neurotic patient on a journey to normalcy ends up driving his therapist crazy. One scene in that movie jumped out at me. Bob is talking to his therapist's daughter about relationships and observes:

"I treat people as if they were telephones. If I meet somebody I think doesn't like me, I say this one is temporarily out of order. You know, don't break the connection, just hang up and try again!"

In my capacity as a pastor, I know a lot of people. I communicate with a lot of people. But I really struggled in the area of *connecting* with people.

The first pastor I ever served with in a full-time capacity was Fred Ward. He had worked as a plant manager in an industrial plant for over fifteen years, and he knew people. I, on the other hand, was hyper-focused on the task at hand; and I had a clear vision of what I wanted to accomplish and worked diligently to make it happen. There was just one problem: if a person got in the way of accomplishing the task, then I would run over them. If they questioned my methods or plans, I often responded poorly. In the end, I got the job done, but the casualties were never worth it. Fred sat me down and said, "Ken, you're just like a surgeon that operates with a chainsaw instead of a scalpel. You get the job done, but you leave a trail of blood and carnage wherever you go!"

He was exactly right. I used the end results (which, by the way, were measurably successful) to justify how I treated people. I didn't listen to Bob's advice. Not only did I break the connection, but on occasion, I ripped the phone lines from the wall!

My mind worked in a certain way that seemed right to me. If I'm doing what I know to be right and being upfront with people, then how can that be a bad thing? If I'm acting in a way that puts the project first and is in the best interest of the organization, then it can't be wrong. If someone doesn't like how I respond, that's their problem, not mine.

Right?

Nope. Wrong.

I was communicating in spades. Everyone was clear about my communication and knew exactly what I was saying. The problem was that what I thought I was communicating was *not* what was coming across. I thought I was communicating leadership and vision. What I was actually communicating was, "I am an insensitive jerk who cares more about projects than I do about people."

My problem was two-fold.

Number one: I needed to learn to truly understand myself. I thought I did, but I didn't. What I thought I was communicating was nowhere near what was being conveyed by not just my words, but more so by my body language, tones, inflections, and eyes.

In the movie *Hitch*, starring Will Smith, the opening segment says something powerful about communication for all of us to consider:

"Sixty percent of all human communication is non-verbal, body language. Thirty percent is your tone. So that means that ninety percent of what you're saying ain't coming out of your mouth."

Are those statistics correct? Some say yes, some say no.[1] I think they're pretty close.

---

[1] https://online.utpb.edu/about-us/articles/communication/how-much-of-communication-is-nonverbal/#:~:text=The%2055%2F38%2F7%20Formula,%2C%20and%207%25%20words%20only

Here was my *huge* problem: I thought my words were enough. I said what I meant—BUT the *way* I said it completely negated my words. Also, the timing of my communication was ineffective.

Rev. William Nevins, a Presbyterian minister in the 1800s, said, "We judge ourselves by our motives, but others by their actions."[2]

That saying is now a little different today: "We judge ourselves by our intentions, but we judge others by their actions."

What does that mean? It means if someone shows up late for a meeting a few times, we instantly label them as chronically late and rude. But if *we* show up late, we give ourselves the benefit of the doubt (traffic, family issue, phone call, flat tire—pick your excuse). We give ourselves the benefit of intent and motive. We take that away from others.

When I was communicating like a complete jerk, believe it or not, my motives were pure. My delivery simply left a lot to be desired. And others were judging me solely by my behavior, which was (to say the least) BAD.

It was at this juncture in my life that I encountered the DISC model of human behavior. In understanding DISC, I (for the first time) actually understood myself. Not only did I understand myself better, but suddenly the blinders were pulled back on people I had judged incorrectly. I got them. I understood them in a deeper way that helped me appreciate them instead of resenting them.

Those same blinders are about to be pulled back for you. You will never look at yourself or others the same way after reading this book. You'll never communicate the same way. But more than communicating, you'll actually be able to connect with those you love and even with those you don't necessarily care for.

---

[2] https://quoteinvestigator.com/2015/03/19/judge-others/

How Jesus Communicated to People Differently When Needed

"But God demonstrates His own love toward us, in that while we were still sinners, Christ died for us. Much more then, having now been justified by His blood, we shall be saved from wrath through Him. For if when we were enemies we were reconciled to God through the death of His Son, much more, having been reconciled, we shall be saved by His life. And Not only that, but we also rejoice in God through our Lord Jesus Christ, through whom we have now received the reconciliation" (Romans 5:8–11, NJKV).

Jesus had a very clear mission. As referenced above, He was sent from Heaven to Earth with the sole purpose of reconciling a fallen world to the Father. Since the Oxford Dictionary defines reconciliation as "the restoration of friendly relations," it is important that we understand how necessary it was that Jesus utilized influence to get people to follow Him rather than trying to coerce them. The Jewish people were accustomed to coercion being used to bring them into compliance, but somehow, this man took a very unique approach. How did this man who didn't rely on station, political influence, or power convince so many people to follow Him, much less as willingly as they did?

Jesus didn't seem to fall into any particular pattern of leadership that could be easily defined.

Some people lead through excitement and a vibrant personality that draws others to them. They are the types who always seem to inspire people with their personal magnetism to join them and their cause. There were times when Jesus seemed to fit this mold. Wherever He went, the crowds always seemed to follow. They couldn't wait to get a glimpse of Him. One day, in Jericho, a man named Zacchaeus climbed up a sycamore tree so he could get a view of Jesus as He came by. When He saw him, Jesus said, *"Zacchaeus, make haste and come down, for today I must stay at your house"* (Luke 19:5b, NKJV). Then Zacchaeus received Him joyfully. There is just something magnificent that happens when someone is recognized, even though they think they are often unseen. The Master certainly noticed him on that day.

Some people lead by building connections and consensus through personal one-on-one interactions. While these people aren't bold, outspoken types, they seem to develop deep relationships fostered by the unwavering sense that they care deeply about and are sensitive to the needs of others. There were times when Jesus seemed to fit this mold.

In the midst of a thronging crowd, a woman who had an issue of blood for twelve years pushed her way through the press of people. (Since she was considered unclean, she knew that she was risking her life for this.) When she touched the hem of Jesus's garment, He immediately turned around and asked, "Who touched me?" Just imagine the bewilderment of His disciples as they saw Him being touched by so many people at once.

When He saw her, why was she in fear and trembling? Because she knew the penalty that she risked with her actions. How did He respond, though? *And He said to her, "Daughter, your faith has made you well. Go in peace, and be healed of your affliction"* (Mark 5:34, NKJV).

Some people lead by pointing out the Law and explaining to others how and why those rules should be kept. They are quick to point out the rules and regulations that are given with the Law. There were certainly times when Jesus seemed to fit this mold as well. In fact, He was very clear when He said, *"Do not think that I came to destroy the Law or the Prophets. I did not come to destroy, but to fulfill"* (Matthew 5:17, NKJV).

Some people lead with a force of sheer will and determination. They are the types who always lead the charge and are driven to achieve the result they're after. There were times when Jesus seemed to fit this mold. In the garden of Gethsemane, where He was betrayed by Judas, a detachment of troops and officers was sent to capture Jesus. Movies and pictures often portray a small squad of soldiers arriving to arrest Jesus, but it is important to note just how determined they were to capture and bring Him in. They had tried to capture Him on several occasions and failed. This time, they wanted to be sure they got the job done. The detachment consisted of somewhere between 300 and 600 well-trained and armed soldiers. In addition, the officers with them were from the temple guard. As the most important religious weekend was upon them, these would have been the elite guard as well. They showed up, confronted Jesus, and got Him to acknowledge that He was the one they were after. Then *Jesus answered, "I have told you that I am He. Therefore, if you seek Me, let these go their way"* (John 18:8, NKJV).

Why is that statement so relevant? Well, they had the manpower with them in that moment to not only capture Jesus, but to take His entire group of core followers into custody all at once, thereby crushing the so-called "rebellion." Yet, in a very direct and bold moment, Jesus told them to let the others go . . . and they DID.

What if . . .

When He saw Zacchaeus, instead of acknowledging him and offering to have dinner with him, Jesus had simply pointed out that he was a filthy sinner in front of the crowd? Zacchaeus would have likely just left, thinking that Jesus was just like everyone else who only saw his faults.

What if . . .

When He felt the touch from the woman in the midst of the crowd, He had turned around and berated her for assuming that she could just come and "take" her healing from Him? How quickly do you think the crowd would have turned on her . . . and likely stoned her to death?

What if . . .

When the religious leaders of the day attempted to point out what was written in the Law of Moses, Jesus had responded with statements about how He felt rather than explaining the deeper meaning of the Law logically to them?

What if . . .

In the garden, instead of demonstrating a command of the situation, Jesus had meekly asked for mercy for His followers? It would have demonstrated weakness and would have likely resulted in the arrest of His entire group of disciples.

Every one of these scenarios could have turned out very differently. However, Jesus was able to relate to each of them the way they needed to be related to in each moment. How did He know? Simple, because he understood how each of them was God-Wired. Therefore, He was able (and willing) to adapt His communication in each situation to help bring about the desired outcome.

While it would be naive to assume there are not good and bad people in the world, it is paramount that we understand each of us was uniquely made in the image of our Creator. Have you ever heard, "You need to be more like him," or "You need to be more like her"? Well, you are not alone. While we certainly can learn to adjust how we communicate with others to help connect and build bridges instead of barriers, we must first begin by acknowledging the unique fingerprint of our soul that God placed in each of us. Psalms 139:14 (NKJV) says, *"I will praise You, for I am fearfully and wonderfully made; marvelous are Your works, and that my soul knows very well."*

Is there any particular personality style that is better or worse than another? Actually, yes. Before you read that and start to think you have a "better or worse" personality style than someone else, allow me to clarify what I mean by that. Your personality style is the one that God chose to give you. Of every possible style, it is the best one for you. He knew that, which is why He God-Wired you the way He did. Whether one personality style is better or worse than another has nothing to do with any style being superior or inferior. It simply has everything to do with whether or not we learn to allow ourselves to operate under control, instead of operating out of control. The great thing is that this is a learnable skill.

Every type of personality God has given to mankind offers some incredible strengths when used properly and under control. Conversely, every type of personality has some very real danger zones when we allow ourselves to operate improperly and out of control. The beauty is that the choice is ours.

We can develop this skill just like we have the ability to develop the fruit of the Spirit inside us as well. As Brian Tracy once said, "Communication is a skill that you can learn. It's like riding a bicycle or typing. If you're willing to work at it, you can rapidly improve the quality of every part of your life."

How Can We Understand Why People Communicate the Way They Do?

There are many different human behavior models that allow us to look at our personalities and how they impact our communication styles. The model we are going to use throughout this book is called DISC. In the pages ahead, we will explain how DISC is used to understand human behavior so you can use it to better understand yourself as well as others around you.

It doesn't take much to realize that we are not all wired the same way. Our goal as you proceed is to help you begin to understand and appreciate the way that you have been God-Wired. It is also to provide a deeper understanding that will help you relate to the differences you see in the personalities of others in your life. Just like you, they have been God-Wired in their own unique way. While no two of us are the same, we definitely fall into patterns.

Scripture makes it very clear that God had no intention of making us all the same. While we are all made in His image, He "wired" each of us differently so that we are equipped to serve the purpose He uniquely crafted for us. Your goal should never be to become more like someone else. It should simply be to become the best version of the person God created you to be. As you do that, you can truly appreciate and celebrate the way you have been God-Wired.

Is your unique style important even if it seems so different from someone else's style? To answer that question, let's close this chapter out by referencing what the Bible has to say about our differences in I Corinthians 12:12–21 (NKJV):

For as the body is one and has many members, but all the members of that one body, being many, are one body, so also is Christ.

For by one Spirit we were all baptized into one body—whether Jews or Greeks, whether slaves or free—and have all been made to drink into one Spirit.

For in fact the body is not one member but many.

If the foot should say, "Because I am not a hand, I am not of the body," is it therefore not of the body?

And if the ear should say, "Because I am not an eye, I am not of the body," is it therefore not of the body?

If the whole body were an eye, where would be the hearing? If the whole were hearing, where would be the smelling?

But now God has set the members, each one of them, in the body just as He pleased.

And if they were all one member, where would the body be?

But now indeed there are many members, yet one body.

And the eye cannot say to the hand, "I have no need of you"; nor again the head to the feet, "I have no need of you."

2

WHAT IS DISC?

Emp and Hip: A Brief History Lesson.

Okay, don't turn the page. Stop. I get it. Some of you don't like history. Yes, I'm a history nerd. BUT—I promise to make this as quick and painless as possible. And it's all *very* relevant in understanding where we're going on this journey to connect with people.

To understand where DISC came from, we have to reach back into the "BCs" to a guy named Empedocles. Yep. I can hear you right now trying to pronounce it. No worries—I didn't have much luck pronouncing his name either the first few times. Let's both be glad you're reading this and we don't have to pronounce it correctly. But I digress…

Empedocles lived in ancient Greece around 400 BC. He developed a theory based on four elements (although he actually referred to them as the four roots): fire, water, earth, air. "Emp" (as he will be affectionally referred to from now on) theorized that everything that existed came from these four roots, and without them, nothing could or would exist. Emp said that everything in existence contained varying forms of these elements in varying degrees. And before we (in our modern era) cast shade on this theory, realize—that theory stayed around for the next 2,000 years. But we're not going to jump ahead that far yet.

Let's fast-forward a few years to a contemporary of Emp. His name was Hip. Okay—Hippocrates. He's known as the father of modern medicine. Hip did a lot to advance medicine in the ancient world, and some of his stuff is still around today. Doctors today still take the "Hippocratic oath" when they begin to practice medicine.

This guy is important to our discussion for one particular theory. Based on Emp's theory, Hip theorized that every human being was made up of four elements in varying degrees. He also said that the amount of each element in a person would determine their overall personality type or *temperament.*

Temperament, noun, *"A person's nature, especially as it permanently affects their behavior."*

Okay, heads-up. This is going to get a little weird. Here are the four fluids Hip told us everyone has:

1. Blood

2. Phlegm

3. Yellow Bile

4. Black Bile

I know. Gross.

Hip theorized that the amount of each one of these fluids within a person's body affected everything from a person's behavior to even diseases in their body. Sound funny? Again—this theory was around for 2000 years too. Think about this: Up until about 200 years ago, people still believed much of this was true. Have you ever heard of leeches being used to cure diseases? That's because doctors of that era determined (based on Hip's theories) an excess amount of blood in a person was harmful and could cause all sorts of ailments.

Yeah, you're probably thinking, but you're talking back in the Middle Ages, right? Nope. As a matter of fact, George Washington, the first President of the United States, ended up dying from this theory in 1799. The doctors determined that too much blood in his system was causing him to be sick, so they started the process of bloodletting to correct the imbalance. In fact, they drained about forty percent of his blood, and George Washington literally bled to death when he was only sixty-seven years old.

Anybody else thanking God for medical advancement?

Back to 400 BC: Hip was the first guy to connect the dots that were essentially four basic types of temperaments. He even named them. Here's how that looks based on Emp's and Hip's theories, based upon which fluid was the most prominent in a person:

1. Blood (Air) was called "Sanguine" and described as a very social or inspiring person.

2. Yellow Bile (Fire) was called "Choleric" and described as a very dominant or aggressive person.

3. Black Bile (Earth) was called "Melancholy" and described as a very sad or avoiding person.

4. Phlegm (Water) was called "Phlegmatic" and described a very steady or supportive person.

Chances are pretty good that you've come across those four terms coined by Hippocrates. They're still thrown around today. The problem is most people can't remember which description goes with which personality style.

It's about to get weirder—consider yourself warned!

Now we come into more of our age. We're jumping from 400 BC to 1920 AD. See? 2000 years of history and you made it! Now we arrive at a man named William Moulton Marston. To say this guy was different would be an understatement. At one point, he was a psychology professor at Harvard. He was (how shall I say this?) morally questionable about more than a few things. He was a polygamist. He lived that way most of his life. I could go on, but you get the idea.

However, he did invent some significant things. He invented the systolic blood pressure machine. That became the basis for what was arguably his greatest invention: the lie detector. As a side note, he also created the comic book character of Wonder Woman. But for the relevance of our discussion, he was the inventor of the modern DISC theory based on some of Hip's theories.

Marston correctly theorized that our personality temperaments had nothing to do with the amounts (or lack of amounts) of fluids in our bodies, but rather every person is simply born (*or hardwired*) with certain temperaments in varying degrees. In his 1928 book,

Emotions of Normal People (we can laugh a bit at him writing about "normal people" later), Marston identified the four basic styles as:

1. Dominance
2. Inducement
3. Submission
4. Compliance

To summarize his theory in his book:

Dominance produces activity in an antagonistic environment.

Inducement produces activity in a favorable environment.

Submission produces passivity in a favorable environment.

Compliance produces passivity in an antagonistic environment.

These theories are the basis of our modern DISC theories today.

Congratulations! You made it through the history lesson. Now let's talk about DISC.

Outgoing or Reserved?

People primarily tend to fall into one of two categories: outgoing and reserved. Let's touch on each one.

Outgoing people have no trouble expressing themselves or their opinions, and they don't really care whether you want their opinion or not. They're normally high energy and intense personalities. They're action takers. This should not be confused with extroverted people. Extroverted people derive their energy from being around people. An outgoing person has no trouble talking, but that doesn't necessarily mean they derive their energy from being around people.

Reserved people keep their opinions to themselves unless they're asked. They're often quieter and have lower energy. They're the ones in the corner not talking very much. They're introspective and more careful. They're great listeners. They should not be confused with introverted people. Introverted people derive their energy from being alone. A reserved person could still derive energy from people while being reserved in their opinions. In other words, they could enjoy listening to people and helping them. A true introvert would find that scenario draining.

In thinking about these two category types and wondering which one you fall into, you might say, "Well—I have qualities from both of these descriptions." I hear you! And you are absolutely right. But—if you had to pick one, even if it's fifty-one percent one and forty-nine percent the other, which one would be the most descriptive of you the majority of the time, when you consider yourself in your most natural and comfortable state?

Circle one: Outgoing or Reserved.

Outgoing

Reserved

Task-oriented or People-oriented?

There are two other category types that people fall into as well: task-oriented and people-oriented. Let's talk about them briefly:

Task-oriented people value projects. They like things to be done. They like to conquer. They like to go through details and ensure that a project is done correctly. They're not there to sit around and have deep conversations; they're there to get a job done. They feel that people need to learn to set aside their feelings and complete their necessary work. When it comes down to a choice between having a conversation and knowing someone or working and getting a job finished, they'll choose the job almost every time. They tend to approach things from a logical perspective.

People-oriented people value relationships. They like to know the people around them. They have difficulty working around people they feel disconnected from relationally. For them, life is much more about the human connections they establish and maintain than the jobs or projects they complete. They feel that people who put tasks ahead of relationships are, at best, insensitive, and, at worst, cruel. When it comes down to completing a task or getting to know someone, they'll choose the relational aspect almost every time. They tend to approach things from an emotional perspective.

There is often a big misunderstanding when it comes to these two category types, which needs to be addressed. Let's begin by being very clear that there is no right or wrong way to answer the "Am I task-oriented or people-oriented?" question. One of these is not better or worse than the other. I have often heard people say something like, "I should probably respond and say I am people-oriented, because if I say I am task-oriented, it might make me sound like a jerk." That is the common misunderstanding that we need to clear up before we go any further.

Just because someone is primarily task-oriented does not mean that they don't love people. It simply means that their main focus is on the task and getting it done. For some, getting the task done effectively is "how" they take care of people.

On the flip side, we need to realize that just because someone is primarily people-oriented, it does not necessarily mean that they love people either. Huh? How can that be? Think about it like this. Someone who is people-oriented naturally focuses on people before the task. People are where their primary attention is.

This is one reason we often remind people that this model of human behavior is referred to as a "values-neutral" model. There is no style or category that makes someone a good or a bad person. In life, we will all inevitably find people who are good and bad (that's just the nature of man) from all different personality styles. Without the understanding that the model is values-neutral, past interactions can skew our future perspectives of people when getting to know them.

Here's an important point: Experience has taught us that roughly ninety percent of all human conflict comes between these two hemispheres. It essentially comes from people disagreeing over which is more important: the task or the person.

So again! You most likely see characteristics of both sides of this equation in yourself, but let's go with our fifty-one to forty-nine percent scenario and ask, if you had to choose, which one would you be?

Circle one: Task-oriented or People-oriented.

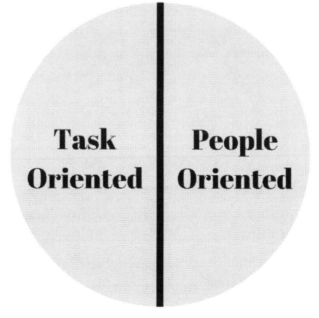

Putting It Together

Okay, let's put together what we just talked about. Some people are more outgoing, while some are more reserved. Which one did you circle?

Some people are more task-oriented; some are more people-oriented. Which one did you circle?

If we divide a circle into four quadrants using these four types of people, we get our DISC quadrant. It looks like this:

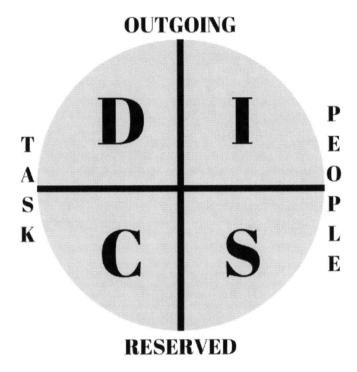

Those who are more OUTGOING and TASK-ORIENTED are primarily a **Driven** type.

Those who are more OUTGOING and PEOPLE-ORIENTED are primarily an **Inspiring** type.

Those who are more RESERVED and PEOPLE-ORIENTED are primarily a **Supportive** type.

Those who are more RESERVED and TASK-ORIENTED are primarily a **Cautious** type.

Let's also say something that we're going to say a LOT in this book—realize that you are NOT simply one type of personality style. One particular style may be your primary style, but you actually have all FOUR styles in you in varying degrees. This is something that Emp, Hip, and William all three got right.

> A D is primarily a more driven and determined personality type.
>
> An I is primarily a more inspiring and influencing personality type.
>
> An S is primarily a more supportive and steady personality type.
>
> A C is primarily a more cautious and correct personality type.

You are going to see these basic personality styles with coworkers—with your family members—and even with those you come in contact with on a temporary basis. You're also going to see them clearly in the lives of the biblical characters we all know and love.

Is this whole thing biblical?

This entire discussion begs the question for believers in Christ: Is this whole thing biblical? The people you described coming up with these theories don't exactly strike me as pillars of Christianity, or even spirituality.

That's a valid question. Let's answer it at the beginning:

YES. DISC is biblical. One hundred percent. You'll see it through-out this book, and you'll see it with the people you're around. You'll see it in the Bible.

But what about these people who came up with these theories? Let's be clear here: They discovered something that already existed. That's what a theory is for. Coming from a biblical worldview, the

Bible tells us in John 1:3 (NKJV, *"All things were made through Him, and without Him nothing was made that was made."*

In other words, not one thing exists in this world that God has not already made. Think of it this way: everything necessary to make an iPhone existed 2000 years ago. The only gap was that man had not yet discovered or theorized the possibility of putting those existing materials together to form what we now take for granted. Many of the people who developed these theories and advanced this technology were not strong believers in the Lord, but today, I scarcely see any person who doesn't own some sort of smartphone device. Who theorized it is not nearly as relevant as whether or not the theory itself holds up to biblical truth.

Does DISC hold up to biblical truth? Yes. In fact, it's based on this verse where Jesus was questioned by the Pharisees and scribes about the greatest commandment from God:

Mark 12:28–31, (NKJV)

Then one of the scribes came, and having heard them reasoning together, perceiving that He had answered them well, asked Him, "Which is the first commandment of all?"

Jesus answered him, "The first of all the commandments is: 'Hear, O Israel, the Lord our God, the Lord is one. And you shall love the Lord your God with all your heart, with all your soul, with all your mind, and with all your strength.' This is the first commandment. And the second, like it, is this: 'You shall love your neighbor as yourself.' There is no other commandment greater than these."

We're going to break down this verse as well as the different styles both in the Bible and in society. In doing so, you're going to discover a great deal about yourself and the people with whom you come into contact on a daily basis.

Ready? Me too, BUT . . . before we go on, let's set up a few quick and painless rules . . .

PART II

Understanding Yourself and Others

A Few Important Guidelines Before We Move On

Before we jump into the "meat and potatoes" of DISC, let's talk about a few rules. I can already hear a few of you saying, "I don't like rules!" We get it. We don't like rules either. We're D-type personalities, and we generally make up rules as we go. In fact, we do it so much that you'll notice this chapter isn't even numbered! That's enough to drive every C personality reading this up a wall! Sorry about that. The I personalities are having fun with this chapter; the S personalities are hoping we didn't upset anyone with our rule breaking (or making!), and the D personalities are thinking, *Yeah, so what? Move on! Get to the point!* But you C personalities should appreciate the "rules" we're about to set.

Okay, the term "rules" still feels bad to some of you, so . . . I'll amend it: a few guidelines. If you were a thoroughbred racehorse, think of these as the fenceposts keeping you safely within the boundaries so you can run with freedom.

There are only five, so this will be quick and painless.

Guideline # 1:

Realize that when you hear about the four temperaments, you're not just one temperament. You're actually a combination of all four in varying degrees.

Have we already told you that? More than a few times? I know! I know! We have! But this point is worth emphasizing again and again because most people miss its significance!

Think of it this way: A car doesn't simply run on gasoline alone. It runs on oil, antifreeze, and brake fluid. We think predominantly about gas because it's what we use the most often and what we refill the most. However, if any of those other fluids are out of whack for too long, your car will be dead, and you'll be on the side of the road calling for a tow truck. (Or you'll be calling your father to come get you sixty miles away at an ungodly hour . . . and I will neither confirm nor deny this from personal experience.)

The same is true of you! You have each temperament in high, average, or low degrees on a scale. What is often missed by so many is that the intensity of the emotions you experience increases as you move further in both directions on the scale. The least intense emotions are found when you are around the average range. The higher (or lower) you move, the more the intensity of the emotions increase, but they do so in different directions. Therefore, it is important to understand when your traits are either high or low. While many brands seem to focus only on your high traits, while ignoring any traits that fall into the lower ranges, we focus on all of them. This provides you with a clearer picture of who you are as a whole person. Where traits fall in the lower areas of a scale, this understanding helps you recognize their importance as well. A "low trait" does not negate its importance in your life.

I was recently in Northern Brazil in Manaus in the middle of the Amazon rain forest. It is where two mighty rivers converge: the Rio Negro (Black River) and the Amazon River. The Amazon River is a brownish color, and the water is fairly warm. The Rio Negro is darker (no big shock there—thus the name) and colder. Here's the thing: when those rivers join together, they don't blend. It's the weirdest sight! The Rio Negro looks like an oil slick intruding upon the brown Amazon. And yet, they run together, side by side.

I actually dove into the Rio Negro and came up in the Amazon. It was so odd. I could feel the cold of the Rio Negro and then the sudden warmth of the Amazon when I crossed into it under the water. So, when I say we are a blend, realize that I'm not saying like red and yellow blending to make orange. I mean blending as in red and yellow are side by side, keeping their individual properties and yet flowing together to paint a truly unique picture.

One weakness I've noticed from some personality models and teaching methods is that they tend to ignore that you are not just one type (or number, depending upon the model). You are more than that number with the "wings" too. Most people who read various personality descriptions honestly will find a little bit of themselves in *every* description. Maybe it's only five percent, but normally there is not one description that defines a person one hundred percent of the time. You're actually a unique blend of DISC traits 1-9 in varying degrees of other models, and to some degree, you are also an E/I, S/N, T,F, *and* J/P in others.

The beauty of DISC is it acknowledges you're actually all four types in varying degrees when taught properly. Yes, I know we even included DISC in the potential weaknesses above, but that is because even with this model, there are those who do not properly understand the nature of our blends and can tend to box people into one area and label them.

Once you know this, you're able to clearly see your weak areas and where your strengths *and* weaknesses are. And when it comes to communication, that's a valuable asset to have.

Guideline #2:

The goal is to learn to speak another temperamental language fluently.

One of the most valuable things a person can do to get a greater perspective on life is to immerse themselves in another culture. When I was in Brazil, everyone spoke Portuguese and very few spoke English. It's a culture shock. It's much deeper than the language, though. You realize that there are cultural differences you know nothing about. Everything from facial expressions to customs.

(A word to the wise: In America, we have a hand gesture that means "Okay"—never do that in Brazil. It does *not* mean "Okay" there!)

One thing that most cultures appreciate is the willingness to learn their language and try to speak it. Many Brazilians *love* to speak English. They practice and practice and then come up to you with a huge smile and say with a thick accent, "Hel-lo! How are you?" When I replied, "I am fine. How are you?" they laughed and said, "I am good!" They were thrilled to communicate. So, I showed them the same courtesy. I learned to say the same thing in Portuguese. When I did, they showed me the same smile.

I'm sure they smiled at me for the same reason I smiled at their accent when they spoke English. If you've ever spoken with a person and heard them speak your language, most of the time, you can pretty much tell if their primary language is yours or not. There is usually anywhere from a slight to a severe accent that reveals whether or not your language is their first or second language.

While you can learn to speak another language, your accent will reveal whether it's your native language. The same thing is true of temperamental languages. I can speak the opposite temperamental language as myself, but it'll always be with a severe accent. It'll also be obvious to the person with whom I'm speaking. They know.

But remember, it's better to speak that language with an accent than it is to not speak it at all. And the more I speak it, the less pronounced my accent will be. The key is to keep learning and keep trying. You will improve over time and will become fluent in all the languages. The interesting thing about the language of DISC (we call it a "language," but it is really a natural communication style that is determined and impacted by our personalities) is that it is universal. If you can learn to speak these four languages, you can effectively connect with anyone in the world.

One of my biggest fears when I'm attempting to speak another language is that I'll mispronounce something and accidentally say something inappropriate. And yep, that's happened to me before. It created an embarrassing situation for me and a humorous situation for the hearers, knowing it was an innocent mistake. But they didn't hold it against me. They laughed, then instructed me in how not to make the same mistake twice. And (thankfully!) I haven't since.

They didn't get mad at me. They didn't walk away from me and never talk to me again. They seemed grateful that I was trying. I've found the same thing to be true with most people when speaking their temperamental language. Most people appreciate the effort. And they are also happy to help you if you make a mistake. *The effort you're making speaks volumes about your desire to connect with them.*

Guideline #3:

Never assume you know another person's language.

Assumption is one of the worst things we can do when we're communicating with others.

Elaine was one of the nicest and most giving women I knew. She was always immaculately dressed and, although she was a true professional woman in a thriving business, she was always willing to volunteer and help other people, especially in their times of need. She had been through a bad marriage and had rebuilt her life as a successful single woman. There was a lot to admire about her.

So, when she came to me and told me she had met a wonderful man whom she wanted to marry and asked me if I would perform their wedding ceremony, I was honored to say yes. Michael was a tremendous guy who loved Elaine. In fact, the look in his eyes when he saw her told me that he adored her. I did their premarital counseling at the church. It was the easiest counseling session I've ever done. They scored the highest of any couple on their compatibility evaluation, especially in the area of realistic expectations about relationships. If any couple was made for each other, it was Michael and Elaine.

We were two weeks away from the wedding; they had completed all of their counseling sessions, and I was eating with my family at a local restaurant. You can imagine my surprise when I looked from my booth to the bar area and saw Elaine sitting cuddled up next to a man who was not Michael.

I got a sick feeling in the middle of my stomach. I looked closer and reasoned on my insides: *Maybe that's her brother?*

Then she gave him a passionate kiss. It definitely was *not* her brother!

I knew I was going to have to confront her. I thought of poor Michael and how devastated he would be when he found out. I began to get angry and thought, *How could she do this to him? He's such a great guy! He loves her!*

I wasn't going to wait for this confrontation, so I got up from my booth and began to walk toward the bar area where they were seated. As I stood up, I saw Elaine stand up with the man, give him another kiss, and, with grasped hands, begin to walk toward the exit. My blood started to boil.

I steeled my courage—I knew this was going to be a very ugly confrontation. Elaine and the man were walking toward me, but they made absolutely no move to avoid me and showed no expressions of shock (unlike my own face!), even though I was pretty sure they had seen me.

I took a deep breath—and as I was almost face-to-face with them, with my index finger of my right hand rising up to point at her in an accusatory manner and the word "Elaine" poised to escape my lips—I felt a tap on my shoulder.

I turned around. It was Elaine.

She grinned broadly and hugged me and said, "Oh, Ken! I'm so glad you're here! Have you met my twin sister, Ellie?"

I looked at Elaine and looked back at Ellie. Then I looked again. I'm pretty sure it was a triple take. They were indeed identical twins.

I looked back at Elaine and replied, "No. I haven't met Ellie, but I've never been happier to meet anybody in my entire life!" A wave of relief washed over me and, after I explained my perspective, they all got a huge laugh out of the situation. I'm happy to report that, over fifteen years later, Elaine and Michael are still happily married and still adore each other.

Elaine was a twin. In all the time I'd known her and in all of those premarital counseling sessions, that little detail had never come up. That was information I could have used that night!

Assuming I knew what was happening almost led me to a humiliating and even devastating relationship faux pas.

I can order a bottle of water in seven different languages. That's purely survival for me when I visit other countries because water is all I drink. One of those languages is Hebrew. I learned to speak Hebrew during my time in Israel. Funny thing—when I speak Hebrew, I'm told I speak it with a Russian accent. Other than "thank you," I can't say anything in Russian. And yet, if someone heard me speak Hebrew, they would assume my native language is Russian, based solely upon my accent.

You can't assume you know another person's temperament based on your own observations. That's because, although actions give you clues and indications, they don't give you conclusive evidence. That only comes through this next guideline.

Guideline #4:

Far more important than a person's action is a person's intent.

We discussed this earlier on, but it's worth mentioning again. You cannot truly know another person's intent. You can only know your own. The best guideline is to give other people the benefit of the intent you give yourself. Give them the same benefit that you would want when you're speaking with them.

Guideline #5:

There is no right or wrong when it comes to our temperaments. There just is.

I've seen people take an assessment and get the results, only to feel like they somehow "failed" it. They don't realize that the assessment isn't a test. It's an *assessment. There is no pass or fail.* The results provide information, but there are no right or wrong answers. The only way you could "fail" a personality assessment is to answer what you "wish you were," or to answer how you think others want you to be. When completing any type of personality assessment, just be true to who you are. Try not to think about how you are in certain environments, because we all adjust to different situations. To be clear, that is completely normal. However, to understand your true style, you need to consider how you would respond to the choices when you are in your most natural state.

You also shouldn't wish that you had a different personality style. The point of this book is that God created you to be the way you are, and you have a unique contribution to make that you and your gifts were uniquely designed to fulfill. Don't despise those gifts! Develop them! Don't wish you had someone else's temperament. Be grateful for your own. You are God-Wired that way for a reason.

Celebrate your own uniqueness. You can work on those weaknesses, but celebrate your strengths. They're there for a reason!

When you read the chapters ahead, you're going to hear some stories and biblical examples from Ken, and you're going to get the in-depth teaching from Chris. Quick secret—Ken is one of Chris's students in DISC. That's right. He learned what he knows about DISC from Chris. Chris is an "Executive Master Trainer" for DISC—a title given by the company, but (and this is Ken talking here), he is also a "Master Teacher" and extremely gifted in taking complex truths and making them simple to digest and understand.

So, in each chapter, you'll get those examples in personal stories and Bible characters as well as important teaching points from the master teacher, Chris. Then you'll get a small recap to help you retain what you've just learned.

One Final Note:

If you are already familiar with DISC, you are probably used to seeing things taught in DISC order. It isn't usually done that way because of any priority system or because there is some kind of "ranking" that suggests any one style is better than another. It is usually just taught like that because that is the order of the letters when it makes the acronym DISC. In this book, we are teaching on each of the four traits, but we slightly changed the order.

You will see these four traits taught in the order of heart, soul, mind, and strength. If this is all new to you, that may not mean a thing. However, for those who are already familiar with the DISC model of human behavior, we didn't want that to potentially confuse anyone. So we felt it was worth mentioning why you will see it laid out differently than it is normally done.

And now that you know what to expect in each chapter, and with those previously mentioned guidelines in place—let's jump into DISC and DISCover how *you* are God-Wired!

Let's dive into the HEART of the matter!

3

LOVE IS A MATTER OF THE HEART

When you encourage others, you in the process are encouraged because you're making a commitment and difference in that person's life. Encouragement really does make the difference.

—Zig Ziglar

Mark 12:28–31, (NKJV)

Then one of the scribes came, and having heard them reasoning together, perceiving that He had answered them well, asked Him, "Which is the first commandment of all?"

*Jesus answered him, "The first of all the commandments is: 'Hear, O Israel, the Lord our God, the Lord is one. And you shall love the Lord your God with all your **HEART**, with all your soul, with all your mind, and with all your strength.' This is the first commandment. And the second, like it, is this: 'You shall love your neighbor as yourself.' There is no other commandment greater than these."*

Yes, the capitalization and bold font were added for effect to make it stand out, but let's start by addressing the heart. It is the first of the four ways in which Jesus instructed us to show our love to God.

Ken's Insights

"You shall love the Lord your God with all of your heart . . ."

Several years ago, I attended a funeral for a wonderful woman who had lived a full life. Her son, a pastor, was delivering the eulogy, and as he was talking, a child in the back of the room was also jabbering away. And I don't mean gently—I mean loudly—as in distracting.

Like most of the people in the room, I was ignoring the noise and just assuming the parent would take the unruly child out, but no. In fact, the child got even louder. Now it was at the point that heads started to turn toward the back of the chapel.

Here is this pastor, in grieving, standing behind a podium in front of a closed casket, delivering the eulogy for his deceased mother, and a parent in the back of the room was letting a child act however they wanted to act! Inconceivable!

And then something happened I absolutely couldn't believe.

The child moved into the center aisle and began hopping like a rabbit toward the front. And the parent never even moved. Yep. As the pastor was preaching. He had been ignoring what was happening, but at this point, he could ignore it no longer. I legitimately felt bad for him in that he was going to have to deal with an unruly child in the middle of such an emotionally gut-wrenching occasion.

The pastor moved to the side of the podium, walked down the steps, and stuck his arms out toward the child. The child immediately ran into his arms.

And then all of us at the funeral service heard him say, "Honey, if you'll let Grandad finish talking, I can't wait to spend time with you and play together, okay?" The child nodded yes and returned to her seat quietly, and the pastor finished the eulogy.

That girl had complete access to her grandfather whenever she wanted. Why? *Because relationship trumps everything else.* When the relationship bond is strong enough, it can overcome anything.

God is a relational God. The entire plan of salvation was done so God could have an eternal relationship with us. To reconcile sinful man to Himself, God sent His only Son, Jesus, to die on the cross in our place, taking our punishment, and providing the way for us to have a personal relationship with Him here on this earth and hereafter in Heaven if we put our faith in Him to be our Lord and Savior.

"Greater love has no one than this, than to lay down one's life for his friends" (John 15:13, NKJV).

The relational God laid down His life for us . . . His friends. If we put our faith in Him, we have a relationship with Him. That's good news! (Which is literally what the "Gospel" means!)

In the Old Testament, David understood this principle. He spent his time in the wilderness tending sheep, playing the harp, singing, and writing love poetry to God. Artistic much? You could say David was an **imaginative** fellow.

He spoke in metaphors to express his emotionally deep and abiding love for the relationship he had with God. David loved being a shepherd and protecting his sheep. He was known for killing a lion and a bear with his bare hands. Is it any surprise, when he described his Lord he loved so much, that he said, "The Lord is *my* shepherd"? In as much as David protected his sheep out of love, he knew God's love for him was much greater, and that his Shepherd would always care for him.

So when this large punk named Goliath showed up on the scene cursing and blaspheming God and striking fear into the hearts of all the Israelites, many of the Israelites were ready to just let this man continue on and take over, but David wasn't having any of it. When others ran away from the giant, David ran toward him.

Why?

Was it because David knew he was stronger or bigger than the giant? Not a chance. Biblical scholars estimate Goliath was about seven feet and ten inches tall.

Was it because David was a better warrior than Goliath? No. Goliath was a well-known, trained Philistine warrior. He was a man of war.

Then why?

David went against Goliath because of his *relationship* with God. He *knew* that the God who had helped him kill the lion and the bear was the same God who would help him silence this giant. He knew God loved him and wouldn't let anything happen to him any more than David would let anything happen to one of his sheep. Some people might call that **impulsive**, but David called it faith.

And David was right. With a slingshot as a weapon and one smooth stone delivered with precision to Goliath's forehead, the giant fell dead.

Inspiring story, isn't it? That day, David gained incredible **influence** with the people of Israel. They were incredibly **impressed** with him, and he became an **important** person in Israel from that day forward. David's relationship with God led him to numerous other victories.

David went heart first. He loved BIG. He was super solid in his relationship with God. David let his emotions overflow and gush throughout the Psalms we still read today. He became the king of Israel; and, to this day, he is known as the greatest ruler Israel ever had. So much so that 3000 years later, the Star of David is still the symbol of the State of Israel.

David is truly the "star" among the Israelites. David was the quintessential "I" temperament.

Let's take a quick break to make an important point:

As we go through the different temperaments, you're going to see many strengths laid out. Each type has strengths, and each type has areas of growth. That's normal. That's a part of it.

Here comes the point:

Every one of our strengths—when pushed out of control— becomes a weakness. Inspiring can turn into self-promoting. Influencing can become manipulative. Impressive can become arrogant. Impulsive can become foolhardy.

So what determines whether it is a strength or a weakness? Easy—WHO is in control? Us or God? When our lives are yielded to the control of God and the Holy Spirit, we can run in our strengths. When we take over and try to do it all ourselves—ugh—look out!

Back to the subject at hand:

Before David became king of Israel, there was another king. He was actually the first official king of Israel.

He was also **impressive** and **influencing**—so much so that the people of Israel demanded that he become their king. His conquests in battle had truly **inspired** the people of Israel. He was tall, good-looking, **interesting**, and, by his physical appearance alone, a very **important** person in Israel.

I personalities are the people we love to see at the front. So when Samuel (the prophet of the time) tried to steer the people of Israel toward God, the people pushed back and demanded a king—one they wanted.

That man was Saul.

Saul did some good things as a king, but he had a weakness. He loved being popular with the people. He loved to be loved by others, and that drove him to do some things that weren't so good.

I's are naturally good connectors. They're the life of the party and the people others love being around because they're so fun and gregarious. That's a strength!

But Saul's strength was pushed out of control, and it led to his downfall. He began seeking the people's opinions and forgot God. He was attacked by an evil spirit, and the only way he could get any relief was for someone (David!) to play the harp and worship the Lord.

Instead of celebrating others, he became consumed with himself. So much so that at one point, the very person who was trying to help him (David) was the recipient of a large spear thrown at him by Saul!

Saul later consulted a witch for advice and ignored God altogether. Eventually, he was killed in battle. His strengths, pushed out of control, led to his death, and David succeeded him as king.

Saul went heart first at the beginning, half-hearted in the middle, and no heart at the end.

And when Samuel talked to Saul about David, he said, *"But now your kingdom shall not continue. The Lord has sought for Himself a man after His own heart . . ."* (I Samuel 13:14a, NKJV).

A man after God's own <u>heart</u>. Wow!

God values those "heart" people, and that is the essence of an "I" personality.

Chris's Insights

Love can't be given without the involvement of the heart. Additionally, to demonstrate love to others requires some form of expression. The feeling of love may be internal, but the expression of it must be external in order for others to recognize it. While Jesus was essentially referencing the passage in Deuteronomy 6:4–7 (He added strength), we know that God is a God of order and never does things by "chance." Therefore, it is very interesting to see that He began with the heart.

When looking at the four personality traits, the heart represents the Inspiring personality type. This is the trait that is primarily outgoing and people-oriented. Why start there? Was it just "luck of the draw"? I don't think so. It was by design because the outgoing characteristic represents being more active, while the reserved characteristic represents being more passive. The Great Commission is a very active (outgoing) and people-focused command. The music group DC Talk said it best in their song, "Luv Is a Verb."

Through years of research, it is widely believed that roughly thirty percent of the worldwide population has the Inspiring trait as their primary trait. The word "primary" is important here because we need to remember that no one is simply one trait or the other. We are all a unique blend of each of the four styles. Even if this is the area you see the least of in yourself, it is important to recognize that there are times you operate within this zone.

Think of it like this: If this is your primary trait, it is like your home address. This is where you tend to go most often and with the least effort.

If it is your secondary trait, this may be where you tend to go when you are under high stress. Unfortunately, we all have to be careful here, because when we begin to operate under our secondary traits in times of pressure, we can also quickly do so in an out-of-control state.

The emotion that is most often tied to this style when it is operating out of control is that of "hate." Kind of like Saul in Ken's example. When you sense that emotion begin to well up within you, allow the recognition of it to help you take a moment, center yourself, and then bring yourself back under control.

But what if this is your lowest trait? I already know what you are probably thinking.

"Here it comes. This is where they are about to tell me I need to 'change' and learn to be more of that."

Actually, nope! I am fully convinced that your unique personality has been God-Wired exactly the way God wanted you to be. And I am certainly not going to tell God that He made a mistake. That said, learning about this style can help each of us achieve greater levels of personal growth and development. Because while it may never be your strength, it helps you to see the need to have people who are naturally high in this area in your life.

Where you once completely misunderstood people with this style, hopefully you now sense that you can better understand them. That is the first step. Over time, you will learn to not only understand them better, but also to appreciate them more. Eventually, you will learn to celebrate them as well.

Before we look at one more example of an Inspiring personality from the Gospels, consider one more thing. Notice how Jesus stated in the foundational Scripture we referenced at the top of the chapter, "with all your heart, with all your soul, with all your mind, **AND** with all your strength." We all have a heart, a soul, a mind, and we have strength. He didn't tell us to pick the one that was our favorite and to love God with that, did He? Of course not. He very clearly instructed us that to love God truly and fully requires us to love Him with all the parts of our being.

Whether the heart (Inspiring personality) resonates with you as your greatest area of strength or as the area you are least inclined to gravitate toward naturally, it is a vital component that makes you who you are. To a greater or lesser degree, it is a part of the DNA of us all. It's just how God-Wired us.

Let's Look At One More Example

One more great biblical example of an I: This guy was a fisherman. But he was more than that; he had many people around him. I personalities attract people. They're magnetic. So, it was no surprise that Jesus found him and gave him the greatest leadership speech in just two words: "Follow me." And he did.

Simon was most definitely an **impulsive** personality. When a storm raged on the Sea of Galilee, he shot his mouth off and said, "Let me come out there and walk on water with you!" And here's the thing—he *did it!* That's **impressive**!

He was one of the three men who had the closest relationship to Jesus on this earth and spent more time with him than anybody else. He was also the one who drew his sword and hacked off the ear of a person who tried to arrest Jesus in the Garden of Gethsemane.

He was even the man who made the most **important** declaration any man has ever made. It was in Caesarea Philippi, when Jesus asked the disciples who people said He was. After they responded that some said He was John the Baptist, some Elijah, and others Jeremiah or one of the prophets, He then asked, "But who do you say that I am?" And for the first time in all of history, Simon looked at Him and said, *"You are the Christ, the Son of the Living God"* (Matthew 16:16b, NKJV).

That day, Simon the fisherman became Peter—the rock. And the confession Peter made became the Rock that Jesus said He would build His Church upon.

But he was also the same Peter whose **interest in people** led him to be associated with a bad crowd outside of Caiaphas's house on the night Jesus was arrested. Peter's **impressionable** personality was pushed out of control that night, and he ended up doing the very thing he said he would never do—denying the Man whom he professed to love and serve.

But he was also the same person who came back from that failure and under the power of the Holy Spirit, **inspired** 3000 people to a saving knowledge of Jesus Christ.

Was he perfect? No way! Neither are any of us.

Peter went HEART first; and, as a result, God used Him powerfully.

To my I-style friends reading this: The same is true of you, my Inspiring friend! You're a rock star! If you have seen yourself in some of these examples, know that you were God-Wired that way. You have an AMAZING personality! Way to go!

4

LOVE COMES FROM DEEP WITHIN THE SOUL

The only way you can serve God is by serving other people.

—Rick Warren

Mark 12:28–31, (NKJV)

Then one of the scribes came, and having heard them reasoning together, perceiving that He had answered them well, asked Him, "Which is the first commandment of all?"

*Jesus answered him, "The first of all the commandments is: 'Hear, O Israel, the Lord our God, the Lord is one. And you shall love the Lord your God with all your heart, with all your **SOUL**, with all your mind, and with all your strength.' This is the first commandment. And the second, like it, is this: 'You shall love your neighbor as yourself.' There is no other commandment greater than these."*

As previously stated, the capitalization and bold font were added for effect to make it stand out, but let's address the soul next. It is the second of the four ways in which Jesus instructed us to show our love to God.

Ken's Insights

"You shall love the Lord your God with all your heart, with all your <u>soul</u> . . ."

Caroline was an amazing administrative assistant. She worked with me for ten years until she was rightfully promoted to greater things. She has a bubbly personality with an infectious laugh. She spreads joy wherever she goes. She is organized and efficient. She is a party waiting to happen. Give her a party to plan and/or a baby to hold, and she is immediately in her happy place.

Although she was fun to talk to, there was also a limit to that talking. People were in and out of her office all the time for the fun and laughter, but when she'd had enough, she told everyone to leave so she could finish her job. After all, she had work to get done, and her sense of duty and desire to accomplish tasks meant there had to be a balance between play and work. If you're reading this in the context of the previous chapter, then you've probably figured out her dominant personality is an I, but her D (which we'll talk about later) was <u>very</u> close behind it!

Caroline did a tremendous job in her time with me. She made life easy for everyone. She made it joyful. She made it fun. She made it organized. Recognizing her was no problem. It flowed naturally. I would stand her up in front of the group and sing her praises; and the people loved her so much that they would often cheer for her, and she ate it up!

My weakness is in administration. Planning out pedantic details stifles my creativity. I can do it, but it's like math for me—it's misery. That's one of the reasons I hired Caroline. She shored up my weaknesses. So, when she told me she was moving on to her promotion, I knew what I was looking for and eventually found it in Kaye.

Kaye is also phenomenally organized; however, she is also much quieter and more introspective. It's not like Kaye to be loud and laughing all the time. She smiles a lot, but she wouldn't consider herself funny. She has an innate ability to hear me say, "I want to do _____" (pick your big project), and her mind immediately goes into action, thinking, *If he's going to do that, it means that I have to do _____* (fill in the blanks with every conceivable detail to get that project done). She's so detailed, in fact, that when I wake up in a panic, thinking, *I didn't tell anyone to do this!*, ninety-nine percent of the time she'll say, "Calm down, Ken—I did that a week ago." She sees ahead and thinks ahead, like any good, thoughtful, efficient organizer does.

The first month she came to work for me, we had a picnic for our group. I could already see Kaye's strength zone in organizing and implementing things, and I wanted her to know how much she was appreciated. Kaye had to run a quick errand to get some more food for the picnic, so I decided to show my appreciation for Kaye in the same way I used to recognize Caroline. I told the group to cheer for her when she returned.

As soon as Kaye got out of her car, with grocery bags in hand, the group cheered her name loudly and clapped and screamed with gratefulness. Kaye's face turned beet red, but she took a bow and smiled. Then she walked up next to me and whispered, "If you ever do that to me again, I'll kill you."

I learned an important lesson that day. Not everyone wants to be recognized publicly. I found out she was grateful when I showed genuine appreciation for her work. But genuine appreciation for her looked vastly different than it did for Caroline. For Kaye, genuine appreciation was in the form of a face-to-face private conversation or, even better, a handwritten note. It showed thoughtfulness in the appreciation and meant more.

Kaye runs like a deep river. People come to her office like they did Caroline's, but at Kaye's desk, they spill their guts. She's one of the best listeners I've ever met. Whereas "I" personalities have a lot of best friends, nearly everyone who talks to Kaye feels like she is *their* best friend. Her ability to listen and truly make them feel valued draws them to her. She believes in deep connections, and her ability to watch, listen, and hear past people's words into the meaning behind them makes her an invaluable connection to most everyone who knows her.

Kaye is an off-the-scale S personality. S styles connect with their souls. Those connections run deep. This is how God connects to us too. The Psalmist who wrote Psalm 42 understood this connection. He wanted something deeper—not a surface connection. He wanted a connection that lifted the depths of his soul to the top of Mount Hermon (that's the highest peak in Israel, by the way).

"Why are you cast down, O my soul? And why are you disquieted within me? Hope in God, for I shall yet praise Him for the help of His

countenance. O my God, my soul is cast down within me; Therefore I will remember You from the land of the Jordan, and from the heights of Hermon, from the Hill Mizar. Deep calls unto deep at the noise of Your waterfalls; All Your waves and billows have gone over me" (Psalm 42:5–7, NKJV).

Jesus had some dear friends in Bethany. Located just a few miles from Jerusalem, Bethany had become a retreat for Jesus. His close friends Mary, Martha, and Lazarus were there. There's an account of an incident in Luke 10. Jesus visits Bethany, and Martha is up working and doing everything while Mary sits at Jesus's feet and is hanging on every word He is saying.

Although Martha didn't like what was happening, Jesus actually commended Mary's choice of sitting and listening. Connecting. As deep calls to deep. As deep connects to deep. Mary connected to her Savior.

The Apostle John also ran deep. He spent time with Jesus one-on-one. He even referred to himself as the "disciple whom Jesus loved," but he never actually attached his own name to his Gospel! The deep connection meant infinitely more than the surface recognition of his own name.

It was John who had a deep enough relationship with Jesus that Jesus entrusted the care of His beloved mother Mary to him and told Mary to consider John as her own son. What a powerful declaration of connection! If there's a more powerful earthly declaration of connection, I don't know it.

S styles know how to have deep bonds that go beyond the surface into the very depths of our souls.

Chris's Insights

Love originates within the depth of the soul. From the moment of our creation, we see God's presence poured into mankind. It started with *"And the Lord God formed man of the dust of the ground, and breathed into his nostrils the breath of life; and man became a living soul"* (Genesis 2:7, KJV).

At the moment that God breathed His breath into Adam, he became a living soul. God placed His essence inside of us. What is that essence? It's love. 1 John 4:16 tells us very clearly that *"God is love."*

Just as an architect carefully crafts the plans for a blueprint, He God-Wired us with a soul. As we have already seen, Jesus then told us that we are to love God with all of it. Some of us tend to communicate naturally from this mode more or less than others based on the unique wiring of our personalities, but the key point to emphasize here is that we all have a soul. Therefore, we need to learn to communicate from that place because we will need it to connect with others effectively, and to be able to fulfill our ultimate calling of spreading His good news to the world.

He started with the heart, but then immediately followed it up with the soul. Just keep that in mind as we continue. We will see the relevance of that when we begin to put it all together in Chapter 7.

When looking at the four personality traits, the soul represents the Supportive personality type. This is the trait that is primarily reserved and people-oriented. People with this style as their primary trait tend to approach things at a slower and steadier pace than those who are outgoing. While someone with a strong Supportive personality style is people-oriented just like their Inspiring counterpart, the biggest difference is often found in their approach to things. Their reserved nature is more like the tortoise in Aesop's fable as compared to the hare, which tends to reflect the fast-paced and outgoing Inspiring types.

Whether this trait represents a natural strength for you or is an area that you don't rate very high in, it is crucial that you understand them and how they relate to others. Why? Quite simply, because research shows that roughly thirty-five percent of the worldwide population has the Supportive personality as their primary trait.

Take just a moment and let that soak in. There are multiple personality style blends. We measure and break them down into forty-one unique designations. Beyond that, there are many variations of intensities within those blends. Our graphs generate nearly 20,000 potential plotting points, which shows the highly unique characteristics of our individual styles.

Ultimately though, we each have a primary style which tends to be our most natural trait. It is the place we tend to go to and operate out of when we are in "cruise control" mode. Even though there are four main traits, this one makes up roughly one third of the population by itself. Yes, this style is the highest percent of the population. This is one reason why it is so important to understand how to connect with people led by this trait.

This style is by far the lowest trait for me. Actually, it is for Ken as well. I realized along my own growth journey that growing, studying, and learning about this style would never cause me to become more of a high S. Remember what I said previously; God-Wired us the way He wanted us wired. Being a high S is simply not a part of my DNA, and it never will be. However, as I have grown and developed over the years, I have learned how to "speak their language" so I can connect with them at a much higher level. That is essentially what this is all about.

As I stated before, if this is your primary trait, it is like your home address. This is where you tend to go most often and with the least effort.

If it is your secondary trait, this may be where you tend to go when you are under a lot of stress. Because we can often find ourselves operating in an out-of-control state in times of high pressure, it is imperative that we recognize what that might look like. The emotion most often referenced to this trait when it is operating out-of-control is "jealousy." When you sense that emotion begin to well up within you, allow the recognition of it to help you take a moment, center yourself, and then bring yourself back under control.

But what if this is your lowest trait? Hey, Ken and I can both totally relate to this one.

In this case, recognize that the natural tendencies of this trait will probably never be your strengths. By the way, that is perfectly okay. This is simply how you were God-Wired. The beauty of this is that when you see the strengths this type brings that you do not naturally possess, you can be intentional about finding people who are strong in this trait to have around you on your team. Doing this will help you see the big picture by enabling you to view the things around you from a different perspective. This only comes when you allow others to help you see how they look from their unique vantage point, as well as your own.

We are going to look at one more example, but before we do, remember the **AND** referenced in the foundation Scripture. The soul is one part of our personality. Just like our body needs all the different parts to be complete, and the church needs all the different gifts to be whole, we need to embrace all the parts of our unique personality in order to express ourselves fully as He intended.

Whether the soul (Supportive personality) resonates with you as your greatest area of strength or as the area you are least inclined to gravitate toward naturally, it is a vital component that makes you who you are. To a greater or lesser degree, it is a part of the DNA of us all. It's just how God-Wired us.

Let's Look At One More Example

The problem that an S faces more than any other temperament is that desire for a deep connection. Connections are great, but remember— if our strengths are out of control, this can lead us to disaster.

This was the case for the woman at the well.

This wasn't just a woman either. This was a Samaritan woman. Samaritans were a mix of Jews and Gentiles. They were generally derided by the people of that day. Also, in that culture, men didn't speak to women who were not family members. Well—at least not a woman with any personal integrity.

Because of that, you can understand when Jesus spoke to her, her response was, *"'How is it that You, being a Jew, ask a drink from me, a Samaritan woman?' For Jews have no dealings with Samaritans"* (John 4:9b, NKJV).

Jesus told this **shy** woman, who was there to get a drink at the well, that He could give her a drink of living water where she would never thirst again. He told her His water gave everlasting life.

So far, we're all on the surface, but Jesus was about to take this to a new level of the soul.

The woman asked for the water, and Jesus immediately spoke to her need. He told her to go get her husband. She gave him a surface reply, "I have no husband."

Then Jesus went right past the surface to the depths of her soul and, as the old saying goes, read her mail. *"You have well said, 'I have no husband,' for you have had five husbands, and the one whom you now have is not your husband; in that you spoke truly"* (John 4:17b–18, NKJV).

The woman was taken aback and realized she was speaking to a Prophet. A Prophet who actually understood her. A Prophet who was speaking to the depths of her soul.

Because of that, her true need came to the surface, and she said it clearly: *"Sir, I perceive that You are a prophet. Our fathers worshiped on this mountain, and you Jews say that in Jerusalem is the place where one ought to worship"* (John 4:19b–20, NKJV).

Her need was obvious. This woman was desperately looking for a true intimate connection with God, but she had no clue how to find it. Because of being stuck and her innate desire to settle for the **status quo**, she was choosing her familiar, **steady** dysfunction and **settling** for less than her God-given birthright, over embracing change and true intimacy. Her lack of intimacy was a function of a lack of a connection with God, which made her insecure.

The advice of men had led this woman astray in her quest for **security**. She was looking for a measure of **stability** in her life. Should she worship on this mountain or that mountain? How could she possibly have true intimacy with God? She had been wasting her life on temporary intimacy with men who had ruthlessly used her, and now she finally stood on the cusp of true intimacy with God. A God she desperately wanted to **connect with and serve**.

Jesus told her who He was: the Messiah. This was a huge declaration. This was an invitation for her to connect her soul to His and be saved.

And she **submitted** herself to the words of Jesus, took that invitation, and was eternally changed. How do I know? Because in John 4:39 (NKJV), John told us, *"And many of the Samaritans of that city believed in Him because of the word of the woman who testified, 'He told me all that I ever did.'"* Because her life was changed by Jesus connecting to her soul, other lives were changed too.

That is the power of a soul's connection to God. That is how God desires to connect to each of us. That is the strength of an S style. They give us the deepest connections to God and to each other. They listen to our needs and speak to them—even when we can't speak to them ourselves!

Deep calls to deep. S personality styles connect with their SOULS.

To my S-style friends reading this: While you don't often seek the limelight or credit, you deserve to be appreciated by all the other styles as much, if not more than, anyone else. You are so often the glue that holds the team together. Your care and concern for everyone else around you represents the core of what true leadership should be all about. We appreciate you.

5

LOVE IS A DECISION OF THE MIND

The difference between something good and something great is attention to detail.

—Charles R. Swindoll

Mark 12:28–31, (NKJV)

Then one of the scribes came, and having heard them reasoning together, perceiving that He had answered them well, asked Him, "Which is the first commandment of all?"

Jesus answered him, "The first of all the commandments is: 'Hear, O Israel, the Lord our God, the Lord is one. And you shall love the Lord your God with all your heart, with all your soul, with all your **MIND**, *and with all your strength.' This is the first commandment. And the second, like it, is this: 'You shall love your neighbor as yourself.' There is no other commandment greater than these."*

As previously stated, the capitalization and bold font were added for effect to make it stand out, but let's address the mind next. It is the third of the four ways in which Jesus instructed us to show our love to God.

Ken's Insights

"You shall love the Lord your God with all your heart, with all your soul, with all your <u>mind</u> . . ."

In all my years of music ministry, David was the best drummer with whom I ever had the privilege of working. I could give him the music and the recording of a song and reliably know that when it came time for the actual performance, it would be right. I'm talking *flawless*. Every tempo. Every hit. Every fill. Everything. It was perfection.

There was a Sunday when a song was done in an improvisational way. That is to say—not rehearsed. Not planned. It was completely spontaneous. David stopped playing midway through. His frustration was obvious. I had a hard time understanding why he was so frustrated. As a drummer, he was the best. I'd seen other drummers who could simply "go with the flow," and I knew David to be more **competent** than all of them.

I was missing a huge element.

David rehearsed the parts I gave him. I recall a few times in rehearsal when he would stop us mid-song and say, "Are we going to do that part the way everyone is doing it now, or are we going to do it the way it's written?"

I thought at first that he was kidding, but he wasn't. He wasn't being a smart aleck either. He truly wanted to know how we were doing that one phrase. After studying DISC, something came into my awareness about David that day that hadn't been there before.

Playing that song in a way that wasn't **correct** or how he had previously rehearsed it *caused him pain.* Attempting to do a song completely on the fly, where people would notice if he made any mistakes, was *beyond painful.* And that pain wasn't David's fault. It was *mine.*

I didn't understand how to properly love him for his mind. Those C personality styles like to be **correct**. Let's get this out of the way at the outset. That does *not* mean they're "know-it-alls"! It simply means they study and prepare so they don't have to be in the wrong. They look at all the angles and possibilities. They rehearse. They prepare. They plan meticulously. And our world is a better place because of them.

Gina (not her real name) was on staff at a church. She served in a support staff position and was one of the hardest workers on the staff. She was one of the first ones there and one of the last ones to leave. Her **consistency** was a shining example to everyone else. When anyone was struggling with a task, Gina would jump in and say, "Let me do that for you!" And she would complete that task extremely well. Suffice it to say, she was one of the most **capable** and **competent** staff members the church had. Staff members referred to her affectionately as "the staff mom."

However, there were a few staff members who didn't seem to get along with Gina. That "staff mom" title wasn't nearly as affectionate with them. One of them told me she was constantly butting into their workday and disrupting their plans with hers. She would interrupt them in the middle of them performing a task, informing them that they were doing it "incorrectly" or in a way that wasn't **compliant** with "best practices," even though it was technically acceptable. It began to cause friction among the staff.

When new ideas were presented to the staff, her systematic mind would **calculate** every possible outcome, and then she would speak up and warn them of the possible bad outcomes of doing the new thing. She questioned every idea to the point that when she would speak up in a staff meeting, the eye rolls from some were obvious. Her questions were meant to get everyone to **consider** the possibilities of harm from certain situations. Her overly **cautious** tone only reinforced her "staff mom" moniker.

In Gina's mind, she was simply helping everyone do things the **correct** way. She had lamented to more than a few people how frustrating it was to have to clean up the "messes" made by others simply because they recklessly proceeded with a task rather than consulting her so she could help them avoid the mistakes.

But if a staff member went to Gina for guidance, coworkers often described her advice as **cold** and without any feeling. Several of her coworkers thought of her blunt answers of the "**correct**" way to do the task as rude and insensitive.

The problem came to a head when her questions were about the senior pastor of the church and the way he had handled an event. He called her in and confronted her about the comments. Her first reaction was to tell him, "I'm just trying to help us do things the right way. You've heard the phrase, 'Measure twice. Cut once'? I'm simply trying to help us avoid doing things incorrectly." And then, attempting to add a touch of humor, she added, "Like any good staff mom would do."

The senior pastor bluntly replied, "With all due respect, Gina, I have one mother, and you're not her. I don't need another mother here. I need a staff member. I need one who supports my vision, even when they don't agree with it. I don't need you talking to others on the staff about how I did something incorrectly. If you have a problem with something I did, you should come directly to me. But you also need to realize that I may not agree with your advice, and if that's the case, I expect you to go with the vision I've laid out."

"Even if it's wrong?" Gina interjected.

The pastor's neck started getting red at this point. He paused for a moment, took a breath, then said, "Gina, have you ever considered that maybe *your* idea could be wrong?"

Gina seemed offended by the question.

"Wrong? No. I've studied and worked very hard to ensure that I'm not. I can actually show you in paperwork and online where the things I've been saying and doing are one hundred percent right."

The pastor interrupted, "That's not necessary, Gina. I've been open to your advice, even though I haven't always taken it. I'm going to say this the only way I know to say this to you: When you become the senior pastor of this church or another church, you'll have earned the right for your vision to be the one at the front. Until then, I need you to follow mine, even if you think it's wrong."

Gina squirmed in the chair and blurted, "I don't know if I'm capable of doing that."

I wish I could tell you the story you just read was made up, but it wasn't. It was a very real encounter, and "Gina" ended up leaving that church, which upset some and made others happy. The saddest part is that the conflict that took place could have been avoided with a greater understanding of how each person was God-Wired and why we process things the way we do.

What the pastor of that church took as mild insubordination by Gina because she questioned the way things were being done wasn't her questioning his authority. It's understandable how that pastor and a few other staff members felt about Gina. She was offering her opinions in areas where they weren't asked for. I call this "Finger in my Fruit Loops" syndrome. Don't put your finger in my Fruit Loops! Especially when I haven't asked you for help!

On a personal note, I (Ken) understand this personality style. Previously, I couldn't say that. My mother was a C. She was overly **cautious**. I remember as a child when I was sick and went to the pediatrician; while I was in the waiting room, I wasn't allowed to play with the toys in the waiting room. Why not? Because Mom told me, "There are germs all over those, and I don't want you to catch something." I, of course, was thinking, *Mom! I'm already sick! Can't I at least have some fun?* But that's what a C style does. They are overly **cautious** and help protect us from ourselves at times. Is it occasionally overboard? Probably. But at other times, they save us from our own lack of vision.

C personality styles are part of the glue that holds organizations together. They are the ones who keep us **compliant** and within the boundaries of the law and best practices. They are the ones who help us avoid painful mistakes.

They also give us incredible details that, while others may consider them to be pedantic, are necessary for us to function properly. Consider for a moment where the Bible would be without the details Dr. Luke gave us in the Gospel of Luke and the Book of Acts. Where would we be without the incredible genealogy that Matthew, the penny-pinching, number-crunching tax collector, gave us? He connected the legal line of Jesus through Joseph all the way back to Abraham! That's some serious ancestral research! We have the internet today, and tracing genealogy back that many generations is next to impossible. It took a strong C with attention to details and meticulous hard work to make that happen.

C styles ask questions. Lots of questions. It's important to understand that asking questions is not challenging authority. They simply must know the answer before they can proceed. To move forward without knowing all the answers is not only painful for them, it's dang near impossible.

Think about questioning. Does that remind you of anybody in the Bible? Maybe ... a disciple named Thomas? He questioned everything. He required proof. So much so, that today, he is known as "Doubting Thomas," even though that title never once appears in the Bible! It's not quite fair, is it? We don't refer to them today as "Murdering Moses," "Adulterous David," or "Denying Peter"! Poor Thomas got a tough break!

His personality style was to question everything. To run headlong ahead without knowing all the pertinent details would be foolish, right? Thomas had to learn that some things require faith that cannot be validated immediately (although Thomas's questions in John 20 were validated by sight in a major way). This is a definite struggle for many Cs.

C styles are **cautious** and **correct** people who help us perform tasks in a **competent** and **compliant** way, **consistently** providing quality work. We need them in our lives.

Chris's Insights

It is impossible to love without involving our mind. Why? Because love is not some feeling that gives us goose bumps. Despite being thought of as primarily an emotion, love is more of a decision that we make. Yes, it is a choice.

"For God so loved the world that He gave His only begotten Son, that whoever believes in Him should not perish but have eternal life" (John 3:16, NKJV).

What was that? It was a decision. Mankind had fallen due to sin, and the law had served to prove that no matter how hard he tried, it was impossible for man to achieve God's standard of perfection that was required in order to be reconciled with Him. But man needed it, and God wanted it as well. His master plan was to redeem all mankind from his failure by providing an acceptable sacrifice that was equivalent to the value He placed on His prized creation, which He had made in His very own image.

Herein lied the dilemma. God is a God of order and justice. Just like someone who has a high C personality type and is represented by the 'mind' in this book, God requires that things be done in a specific order. He doesn't have integrity. He *is* the literal image of integrity. If he were to purchase man back from his fallen state by paying less than his value, would He then still be a God of justice? He only had one real choice. Because He placed so much value on us, He had to pay for us with the only thing He had that could equal our value in His eyes. Not even the angels could qualify for that. It would require His own Son.

The choice was made. The plan that was put in place from the foundation of the world was in full motion. Jesus had spent three and a half years conducting His earthly ministry and was preparing for the final act. He was preparing for far more than simply a crucifixion. He was about to take on the sin of all humanity upon Himself and knew that act would cause His Father to have to turn from Him. In all of time and history, He had never known separation from His Father, but the time was now imminent. And to think that so many people really think He was struggling so hard because of the simple physical abuse that was to come. That was nothing compared to the pain of separation from His Father. Did He want to do this?

"He went a little further and fell on His face, and prayed, saying, 'O My Father, if it is possible, let this cup pass from Me; nevertheless, not as I will, but as You will'" (Matthew 26:39, NKJV).

What we see here was a conscious decision of the mind. I have no doubt that He was using all His heart, soul, and strength in this moment as well, but this required Him to commit to the plan of the Father. That simple statement, "if it is possible" lets us know that His mind was searching for another way in that moment. But He knew there was no other way, so He made a decision (mind) to follow through with the plan.

Aren't you glad He did? I certainly know I am. I am not even qualified to pay for my own sins, much less for everyone else's.

He started with the heart and then went to the soul. Each of those addressed the internal core of who we truly are. The third area He told us to love God in was our mind.

While looking at the four personality traits, the mind represents the Cautious personality type. This is the trait that is primarily reserved and task-oriented. This is the trait that helps us ensure we do things the right way.

Remember when Ken shared above about that guy who is often called "Doubting Thomas"? I sometimes wonder why he was given such a nickname. Oh, I know the stories, but it just seems like it is too easy for those of us who are reading them to criticize him for questioning the way he did. Because, "of course," we would *never* have done that if we had been there. (I truly hope you sense the sarcasm in that last comment.)

While I fall in the average range of this personality style, neither in the high nor the low segments, I have a true appreciation for Thomas specifically. I find it interesting that while people today often call him a demeaning name, Jesus never once corrected him for his nature. Perhaps that is because He knew the way Thomas was God-Wired and understood that he was just the way God intended him to be.

I know, Jesus told him to touch His wounds with his hands and to believe. But He did not chastise him for it. As someone who did not become a Christian until I was an adult, even before I began to study human behavior, I recognized something unique about Thomas. He was cautious. He was not about to go and die a martyr's death over something he was not fully convinced of. The fact that he was so sure that he was willing to die for the cause was a big reason I was convinced of the validity of the Gospel.

So, on a quick side note to all you reading this who are high C personalities, know that I am being sincere when I say I am truly grateful that you all are the way you are. You are totally awesome in my book!

Now, let's see where you fit in the grand scheme of things. Roughly twenty-five percent of the population has the Cautious type as their primary trait. It makes total sense though, right? Just think about it for a minute. As a high C once said to me after giving a speech on human behavior, "There are four personality styles. You would think each of us would make up about twenty-five percent, but apparently, we were the only ones who got it right. The other three styles all got it wrong."

I still chuckle to this day when I think of that. I actually thanked him for proving everything I ever said about high C personalities to be correct with that single statement. You just can't make this stuff up. It's priceless.

As previously noted, if this is your primary trait, it is where you tend to go most often and with the least effort.

If it is your secondary trait, this may be where you tend to go when you are under a lot of stress. Be cautious here (pun intended), because the emotion that is most often referred to this style when it is operating out of control is that of "fear." They get so scared of making a mistake that they make the biggest one of all, which is doing nothing.

If this is your lowest trait, understand that you will probably never truly understand why people like this need everything to be so precise all the time. But as I remind audiences often, I am always thankful for all the high C personalities God saw fit to put on this earth, especially every time I drive over a bridge or find myself 30,000 feet above the ground in a giant metal tube. We can all certainly find a real quick reason to be genuinely grateful for their attention to detail then.

Let's Look At One More Example

Moses is one of the most well-known people in the Bible. He led the captive Israelites out of bondage in Egypt. He crossed the Red Sea on dry ground. God entrusted him with the Ten Commandments. He led the Israelites to their Promised Land. With five books and one Psalm, he wrote more of the Bible than any other man. There are 125,139 words of the Bible credited to him.

And yet, Mr. C personality, Mr. **Compliance** with the law, Mr. **Consistency** in his leadership style had a major flaw. He was doing everything himself. I mean, why wouldn't he? Who could possibly do the job as well as he could?

"If you want it done right, do it yourself!" That mindset is a fatal flaw for many C styles.

It minimizes your effectiveness and your leadership.

Moses is operating with what he considers to be good leadership. He's teaching everyone the law. He's making sure everyone stays in **compliance** with the law. He is **cautiously** keeping the Israelites from harming themselves and keeping them safe from attackers. He is extremely **consistent** in all his leadership. He is **careful** with how he handles his interactions with God and with the people. You would think this would be stellar leadership.

But it wasn't.

One day, Moses's father-in-law, Jethro, showed up and had a conversation with Moses. Moses recounted—in great detail, I might add—all the wonderful things God had done and how God had used him to accomplish some phenomenal tasks. Jethro listened and commended him.

But then, Jethro got to the crux of their meeting in Exodus 18. Jethro watched Moses sitting day and night judging the people. No, that doesn't mean he was judging them as in criticizing people who walked around. It meant people were bringing him disputes they couldn't decide for themselves, and he, according to the Law of God, would judge what was right and wrong for them.

Jethro questioned Moses on it in Exodus 18:14–18 (NKJV):

"So when Moses' father-in-law saw all that he did for the people, he said, "What is this thing that you are doing for the people? Why do you alone sit, and all the people stand before you from morning until evening?"

And Moses said to his father-in-law, "Because the people come to me to inquire of God. When they have a difficulty, they come to me, and I judge between one and another; and I make known the statutes of God and His laws."

So Moses' father-in-law said to him, "The thing that you do is not good. Both you and these people who are with you will surely wear yourselves out. For this thing is too much for you; you are not able to perform it by yourself."

Did you catch that? Doing everything yourself not only wears you out, but it also wears out the people you're supposed to be leading!

Moses was using his strength! He was helping people stay **compliant** with the law and do things **correctly,** but (ironically) he was doing it in the wrong way. This is a perfect example of a strength zone pushed out of control.

Jethro then helped him learn the fine art of delegation, and it helped Moses as well as all of Israel. We would do well to learn the same lesson.

C personalities have a strong tendency to do everything themselves out of a desire for it to be done "right," but this type of leadership demotivates the people we lead. It also creates a vacuum when that person leaves leadership in that nobody is equipped to do that job. That is one of the worst places we as leaders can be. In fact, if we aren't currently training, mentoring, and empowering someone (or multiple people) to do what we are currently doing, then we're not truly fulfilling our calling as leaders.

C personalities lead with their minds. They're logical. They're systematic. They're extremely **conscientious.** They're **consistent**. You can always count on them.

We desperately need them. They are the glue that holds organizations together.

To my C-style friends reading this: God certainly knew what He was doing when He God-Wired you the way you are. And whether some people realize it or not, we are all much better off because of you. Thank you for your attention to detail, which constantly helps us turn our good ideas into great outcomes. We could not do it without you.

6

LOVE DEMONSTRATES STRENGTH

When your dream is bigger than you are,
you only have two choices: give up or get help.

—John C. Maxwell

Mark 12:28–31, (NKJV)

Then one of the scribes came, and having heard them reasoning together, perceiving that He had answered them well, asked Him, "Which is the first commandment of all?"

*Jesus answered him, "The first of all the commandments is: 'Hear, O Israel, the Lord our God, the Lord is one. And you shall love the Lord your God with all your heart, with all your soul, with all your mind, and with all your **STRENGTH**.' This is the first commandment. And the second, like it, is this: 'You shall love your neighbor as yourself.' There is no other commandment greater than these."*

As previously stated, the capitalization and bold font were added for effect to make it stand out, but let's address the trait of strength next. It is the last, but definitely not least, of the four ways in which Jesus instructed us to show our love to God.

Ken's Insights

"You shall love the Lord your God with all your heart, with all your soul, with all your mind, and with all your strength."

I heard Heisman Trophy Award-winning quarterback and NCAA National Champion Tim Tebow interviewed recently. He talked about coming to the United States (his parents were missionaries to the Philippines, and he was born there) and then being enrolled in a children's sports league and playing in a T-ball game. His coach told the team, "Remember, kids—it doesn't matter whether we win or not. Just have fun."

Tim, who was part of a competitive family, spoke up and said, "That's not true. It is about winning. Winning is fun." He was pulled aside by his coach and told that his attitude was wrong. The coach spoke to Tim's father and told him the same thing. Tim's father (Bob) told the coach he would speak to him and walked over to Tim and said, "It's Okay, son, he doesn't understand us."

Tim then told the audience, "I've always wanted to compete and win. I guess you could say I've always been a **driven** personality." In fact, Tim often wears a shirt that says "**Driven**" on it.

That is the essence of a D personality. They're **driven** to succeed. **Driven** to win. **Driven** to conquer whatever challenges lie in front of them. They face challenges **directly**, head-on.

During the first century, the newly formed church in Corinth, Greece, was a mess. A big mess! There was dissension, arguing, and rampant immorality. The Apostle Paul came to the rescue with two scathing letters we now call I and II Corinthians. He spoke to the church with a little bit of encouragement in the first part of the letter and a little at the end, but the middle was beyond direct in its assault on the issues this church was having.

The church was having trouble discerning the difference between right and wrong. They needed **decisive directions** to give them the needed guidance.

In many ways, there are some who would consider Paul's writing to be rude. Others would say they appreciate the straightforward approach. The mess in Corinth merited a strong response, and that's exactly what happened with Paul's D personality—a strong as garlic, **direct**, **dynamic** response that **demanded** a change in action.

Another great biblical example of this temperament was in the town of Bethany. We've already talked about Mary, the sister of

Lazarus, who sat at the feet of Jesus, intently hanging on every word he said. But what about their other sister, Martha?

Martha was **determined** not to be the only one serving. She actually scolded Jesus! *"Lord, do you not care that my sister has left me to serve alone? Therefore tell her to help me"* (Luke 10:40b, NKJV).

In other words, she was saying, "Jesus! She's not **doing** anything! She's just sitting there!"

Of course, Jesus pointed out that by sitting there listening to Him, she actually was **doing** something. In fact, what she was **doing** was the most important thing she could do.

D styles are natural **doers**. They don't value words without action. And they definitely don't value inaction. Their strength moves organizations and people forward. Without them, projects and organizations have a way of stalling out or suffering, often from what is commonly known as "analysis paralysis."

Chris's Insights

For love to be given genuinely, it requires that we freely give it from our strength. You simply can't give what you don't have. When we lack something, we need it in our lives. Can you then give it away? No, because you don't currently possess it.

Strength comes from that which we possess. If we have something, we can choose to give it away. That is because we are operating from a position of strength. Love operates much the same way.

I am going to speak bluntly for a moment. I am an extremely high D, by the way. Besides, this is the chapter written for the Driven personality type, so if this fits you, then you know exactly where I'm coming from.

The truest test to determine if someone is truly giving love is to see if they give it when they know the person receiving it has nothing they can offer in exchange. God gave His Son Jesus to redeem us because He loved us and wanted to restore the relationship with us that existed at the beginning, before sin separated us from Him.

What could we offer in return? Of course, we can give Him our love and our worship. But let's be real. He is God and will sit on the throne, whether we do or not. It's not like He is not going to be God if, for some reason, we said no to Him.

I'll give a more practical example. Have you ever had someone you cared about who you wanted to help anytime you could? This person might have been a family member, a friend, or someone you were close enough to that you considered them a brother or a sister to you. You really felt like they loved you and cared about you the same way you did for them. Then something unexpected occurred. When it seemed like they were no longer "benefitting" from you, they stopped being there for you. What caused that? Their "love" was very conditional. It was not being given from a position of strength. It was only being offered from a position of need. As long as they got something from you, they were right there with you, but the moment they weren't experiencing the benefit they expected from the relationship, they seemed to vanish.

I know that was a harsh example, but we have all been there at one point or another. Remember, I have already shared that I am a very high D. I am willing to give love from a position of strength because that is my choice. However, I will not have it taken from me.

Before you start to think, *That's super harsh, Chris!*, let me share exactly how Jesus said it.

"Therefore My Father loves Me, because I lay down My life that I may take it again. No one takes it from Me, but I lay it down of Myself. I have power to lay it down, and I have power to take it again. This command I have received from My Father" (John 10:17–18, NKJV).

"Or do you think that I cannot now pray to My Father, and He will provide Me with more than twelve legions of angels?" (Matthew 26:53, NKJV).

That response in Matthew was given to Peter in Gethsemane when Peter tried to stop them from arresting Jesus. I can imagine what Heaven must have looked like at that very moment. Not even the angels fully understood God's redemptive plan. I can picture the archangel Michael standing with the legions of angels at his command. He was probably listening intently for Jesus to simply utter a word. He could have simply said, "No more," and it would have been over. But Jesus chose, from a position of strength, to fulfill the task at hand.

When looking at the four personality types, strength represents that Driven personality type. This is the trait that is primarily outgoing and task-oriented. This style is extremely action-oriented and lives by the motto, "Let's do this!" Is it any wonder why God used someone like the Apostle Paul to single-handedly write so much of the New Testament and to be so active in spreading the Gospel during the early years of the new covenant church? His "All go, no quit" personality was perfect to lead the task at hand. Gee, it's almost like he was God-Wired for this specific purpose. Hmm! Imagine that!

Research tells us that this is by far the smallest percentage of the population. The Driven personality type only makes up roughly ten percent of the population. Before you start thinking, *Well, that's not fair*, hear me out. Because this style is often so strong in their approach, that is probably all we could handle! Think of us as a great spice when cooking. We can definitely add some great flavor, but too much would ruin the meal. It would just overpower everything else.

My wife says often that she is convinced the reason God (in His infinite wisdom) made us by far the smallest percentage of the population is because there are too many "red buttons" in the world. She says it is only funny because we know it's true.

While we all have this trait, like every other trait, to some degree, through years of studying human behavior and training people from all over the world, I can see why the smallest group of all the styles as their primary trait is the Driven style. Because we can naturally get results better than anyone, but we have to be so careful not to run over good people in the process and end up causing more harm than good along the way.

I get it. You may be thinking, *Someone got their feelings hurt, but we got the job done. That was what really mattered.* Not only is my

Driven trait the highest possible plotting point on the graph, but I was also an M1 Tank Commander during my time in the military. In that job, everything relied on me to make the call and take action very quickly. But I also remember my first corporate job when I was leading multiple stores. My VP, who I will always value as a mentor to me when I needed it, said something I needed to hear one day. I'll never forget his words.

"Your numbers are great, Chris, but this isn't the Army. They don't have to show back up to work tomorrow morning."

Those words stung, but I needed to hear them. I truly cared about my team. In my mind, getting great results was how I was taking care of them and their families. But his words helped me to see that I could accomplish so much more by building a team of "we" rather than "me."

Just like the other traits showed, if this is your primary style, it is where you tend to go most often and with the least effort. It is how you operate when you are on cruise control in your life.

If it is your secondary trait, this may be where you tend to go when you are under high stress. Because we can often find ourselves operating in an out-of-control state in times of high pressure, it is imperative that we recognize what that might look like. The emotion most often referenced to this trait when it operates out of control is "rage." Yikes! When you sense that emotion begin to well up within you, allow the recognition of it to help you take a moment, center yourself, and then bring yourself back under control.

But what if this is your lowest trait? In this case, recognize that the natural tendencies of this trait will probably never be your strengths. By the way, that is perfectly okay. This is simply how you were God-Wired. The beauty of this is when you see the strengths the Driven style brings that you do not naturally possess, you can be intentional about finding people who are strong in this trait to have around you on your team. Doing this will help you see the big picture by enabling you to view things around you from a different perspective. This only comes when you allow others to help you see how they look from their unique vantage point—as well as your own.

Let's Look At One More Example

God blessed Samson. We know God's hand was on him because the Bible tells us "The Spirit of the Lord began to move upon him," which is a pretty amazing thing in the Old Testament.

There's something you'll notice about Samson pretty quickly in Judges 14. He liked to be in charge and **dictate** what was happening. He was **demanding**. He was ordering his parents and everybody else around, and they complied with his **directives**.

Samson was phenomenally strong. So much so that he tore a lion apart with his bare hands. I'd call that very strong.

We also know he was intelligent. He was posing riddles to people to get the things he wanted. The thirty men to whom he posed the riddle used Samson's wife to trick Samson into telling her the solution, which she then went back and told the men.

Want to talk about being **direct**? Look at his reply to the men who "solved" his riddle in Judges 14:18b (NKJV): *"If you had not plowed with my heifer, you would not have solved my riddle!"*

Anybody know of any other husband who could get away with that statement and still be alive that day? He said what he meant, and he meant what he said; and he didn't really care if he hurt anyone else's feelings if he said it.

The other thing about him was Samson was indeed a **doer**. After **directly** castigating the men who had used his wife to get their way, he killed all of them. His actions spoke for themselves. He was **driven** to win and conquer.

In the next chapter, after a series of tragedies that affected him, Samson killed one thousand men with the jawbone of a donkey. Just wrap your head around that for a second: The battle was *one thousand vs. one,* and he killed them *all*. He carried a city gate up a hill. Samson embodied strength and victory. Talk about a **dynamic** personality! He was a Bible superhero!

But he had a fatal flaw.

The desire to win and conquer can be a positive for a D personality, but in Samson's case, this desire got way out of control. In his desire to conquer and win, he had a weakness to conquer women. The Bible is clear that Samson's weakness for women caused him to sleep with many of them. It also caused him to be manipulated by them in order to get what he wanted, which was a physical relationship with random women.

Samson ends up with a devious woman named Delilah, who, for a nice payday from the Philistines, betrayed Samson. She manipulated him to tell her the secret of his strength (his Nazirite long hair), and it cost him everything.

This Bible passage contains what I believe to be one of the saddest moments in all the Bible. It's in Judges 16:20b (NKJV): *"But he did not know that the Lord had departed from him."*

In trusting in his own strength and forgetting the Source of that strength, his confidence turned into arrogance, and he lost his life.

But this D personality left with a statement that showed his dogged **determination**. After he lost his strength, he was blinded by the Philistines and used as entertainment for them, but at the end, while standing in the temple, he remembered the Lord and regained his strength enough to push the supporting pillars of the temple down; and he killed more Philistines in that one moment than he had in his entire life.

This story reads like a Shakespearean tragedy, and it serves as a warning.

When we trust in our own strength and start to believe our own press, we're diminished.

Jonathan (not his real name) was the CEO of an organization. He was **dynamic** in his leadership. He was **diligent** in his duties. His strong **drive** kept the company at the forefront of their industry. He had huge **dreams** and was **determined** to see those dreams become a reality.

But like Samson, Jonathan had a problem. No, it wasn't women.

Jonathan's problem was that he was doing well, and his desire for success and his determination to succeed at all costs caused him to put everything on himself and run over the people who were working so hard to make everything happen. They, too, shared the burden of wanting things to be right and succeeding in their industry, but they felt unappreciated, stepped on, and they'd had enough.

Enter Scott into this picture (again—not his real name). Scott was also a D personality, who had zero trouble with confronting anyone. Scott was a vice president at the company who had the ear of others in the organization. Scott took it upon himself to take the complaints of the people to the board of directors. When Jonathan found out, he immediately fired Scott, but the board of directors, after confirming that some of the complaints were valid, voted Jonathan out and brought Scott back in as the new CEO.

Scott began leading the organization, which was honestly what he wanted all along. He thought he should have been in charge years ago. But the sudden turn of events caused a turnover in the company, and their productivity that had been soaring started to decline for the first time in years. Within eighteen months, they were at about half of their previous productivity. Scott ended up resigning and moved to a support position in a different company, where, inexplicably, he continued the same pattern of thinking that he should be in charge instead of the CEO.

The truth is two-fold here.

1. Scott should've addressed his concerns directly with Jonathan, but he didn't because his goal wasn't for the company to get better. His goal was to take over and to be in charge at any cost.

2. Jonathan was the right person for the job, but he needed people around him to tell him the truth. He also could have grown by learning to listen, learn, develop, and make the proper adjustments.

Bold leaders like D types need strong accountability, and the most important lesson they can learn is this: **before you can be in authority, you have to learn to properly be *under* authority.**

To my D-style friends reading this: You may represent the smallest group of people on the planet, but you are definitely the movers and shakers who know how to get things done. You bring energy, drive, and determination to win with you wherever you go. Allow God to help you hone your desire to achieve results with a clear focus on helping the entire team achieve more than they ever thought possible. When you do that, you amplify one of the greatest strengths He put in you. Hey, my friend, it is what you were God-Wired for. Own it!

7

Putting It All Together

No matter how clear you think your message is,
until they truly understand,
you haven't achieved communication yet.
Effective communication is the art of getting through.

—Chris Rollins

To this point, we have taken you on a journey that has provided a brief overview of what DISC is all about. Then we dove into each of the four traits individually, as they are represented by the heart, soul, mind, and strength.

We have repeatedly mentioned (and will continue to drive the point home) that you are not merely one style or the other. You are a unique blend of all four traits. You have a primary style, which is likely the one you seemed to resonate with most quickly as you read about each in their previous chapters.

More than once, you might have even caught yourself saying, "Hey. That one really fits me too!" No, that doesn't mean you got confused. It simply means that you are probably high in more than one area. We completely understand. Both of us are extremely high in two of the four traits on the graph.

I would love to say that the DISC model always helps people understand their entire blends so they can learn to appreciate the way they were God-Wired. Trust me when I say I even contemplated whether to say this in the book, but I would be doing you a disservice if I left it out.

DISC is simply a model that was developed to help us learn to understand ourselves and others better. When I hear people say, "Well, all DISC is the same," I just shake my head. Pick any profession and any topic in the world. Why would someone pick one college over another? I've heard people say they picked one college because they had an amazing reputation for having a high-quality engineering program. Hmm? So should I assume then that all engineering programs aren't the same? I could provide a thousand examples here, but I think you get the point.

I am going to take a moment to throw in a shameless plug for my coauthor Ken. One of the things I love about Ken, and part of why I decided to write this book with him, is his desire to do the work it takes to be great in his profession. He is a high D, so I know he wants results. But because he operates under control, he understands that he can make a greater impact on the Kingdom by helping others create stronger teams that work well together.

Ken has literally spent at least 100 hours in live training sessions with me to continue to learn and develop. While he is an Advanced Human Behavior Consultant, I know he has also continued to learn and develop his understanding of this model through hundreds of additional hours of ongoing lessons, as well as time spent teaching and speaking on it. Let's face it, anyone can get "certified." Ken fully embraces my challenge to those I teach to put in the personal effort required to actually be "qualified." Trust me when I say there is a HUGE difference. Okay, back to the task at hand...

There are those (like Ken) who have invested the time and effort to really learn and master their craft. Then there are those who looked for the easiest and quickest way to get the credentials they think will help them get by.

Why does that matter to you? It matters because we have all encountered people who had the _____ (license, degree, certification, etc.), yet they didn't seem to be qualified to do what they were doing. In DISC specifically, I have seen people countless times through the years focus only on someone's high traits while completely ignoring their low ones. In fact, I have even been guilty (because it was what I was taught years ago) of saying I have "a lot" of one trait and "almost none" of another. In reality, nothing could be further from the truth.

If I had to point out one of the biggest take-aways I have learned from Dr. Rohm through the years, it has been the focus to point out our true blends of unique styles. Our high traits carry with them a level of emotional intensity. But guess what? Our low traits tend to do the exact same thing. The traits we are very low in have just as much to do with how we were God-Wired as our high traits do. The intensity is just in a different direction.

While our graphs that are created when someone takes an assessment can be broken down several different ways, one simple way to view them is to see areas where we are high/very high, average, and low/very low. Interestingly enough, the ranges where we tend to have the least emotional intensity are not in the low areas. They are in the average ranges. These are the areas where we are typically the most flexible and can truly go either direction as needed without too much effort. Because we are not very high or low in those areas, we won't stay there, though. We simply flow there when needed; but then, we tend to revert to our natural zones.

See, I told you there was more to it. So, if you have ever felt labeled or "put in a box," hopefully, as you are reading this, it helps you realize that is not our goal at all.

I remember a full day training session at a college where we were training the staff. Bill (not his real name) didn't want to be there, and it was completely obvious to everyone in the room. He sat in the session from the start of the morning with his arms crossed and barely said a word, even though we tried to engage him. He made it known early on that he had "done DISC before" (his exact words).

I will never forget as we were preparing to break for lunch that day, because he decided then that it was time to speak up. He wanted to address the room for a moment. I remember thinking, *Oh great! Here we go.* What he said next, though, not only shocked me, but it also reinforced in me just how important it is to understand the blend of our styles.

He started by saying, "I didn't want to be here today." (Gee, what a shock that *wasn't*.) Then he reiterated what he had said earlier about having "done DISC before." But you could almost hear an audible gasp across the entire room when he said, "When I went through this before, I felt like I was labeled, and I don't like that. During this session this morning, for the first time, I have felt understood." Needless to say, it was like having a completely different person in the session with us that afternoon.

I didn't tell you that story for any type of credit. I simply want to drive home the value of truly understanding this model and how it can help you and your team embrace the way that each of us has been uniquely God-Wired so we can unlock our true potential within.

In Part II, we took a deep dive into understanding each trait. The primary focus of that was so you could each learn to understand yourself. Remember, you can't learn to love others properly until you first learn how to love yourself. Listen, we are definitely not referring to narcissistic behavior here. That is a completely different issue. We are simply addressing the fact that so many people fail to appreciate themselves for who they are. If that is you, perhaps it is because you haven't *yet* learned to appreciate the way you were God-Wired. When you learn to love and value yourself properly, you honor God by acknowledging your appreciation of His design, because it was God who made you the way you are. Regardless of your personality style, you were made in His image. Oh, and by the way, any of the greatest masterpieces we see throughout history pale in comparison to God's works of art (YOU).

"For we are God's masterpiece. He has created us anew in Christ Jesus, so we can do the good things He planned for us long ago" (Ephesians 2:20, NLT).

Now, before we move on to Part III, where we begin to look at each style again and understand ways we can adapt to communicate effectively with them all, let's first take a look at some of the characteristics these traits have. This will help us find where commonality exists between styles, and even how you can flow to connect to the area that is often the hardest for you to relate to.

Let's take a look at the traits one more time.

Driven (represented by the strength)

Inspiring (represented by the heart)

Supportive (represented by the soul)

Cautious (represented by the mind)

Back in Chapter Two, you were introduced to these. We also explained the four characteristics that help define these traits. We have Outgoing, Reserved, Task, and People characteristics. As you are about to see, recognizing these can help you understand others who are not necessarily like you by seeing the areas of focus that you have in common.

Outgoing

Both the Driven and Inspiring styles share this characteristic in common.

Reserved

Both the Supportive and Cautious personality styles share this characteristic in common.

Task

Both the Cautious and Driven personality styles share this characteristic in common.

People

Both the Inspiring and Supportive personality types share this characteristic in common.

Keep in mind that we all have the ability to "flow" from one style to the other as needed. This is not changing who we are, but rather adapting as situations call for it in order to connect and communicate with others effectively.

For example, my highest trait is the Driven style. When communicating with an Inspiring personality style, I know we are both outgoing. That becomes the "connecting point" I use to help us get on the same page. When communicating with a Cautious personality style, I know we are both task-oriented. That becomes the "connecting point" I use to help us get on the same page.

But what about the Supportive style? My style is outgoing and task-oriented, while theirs is reserved and people-oriented. There doesn't seem to be any commonality here. Well, this is why our focus on your blend becomes so important. While my "primary" trait does not share any characteristics with them, my secondary style is Inspiring. Think of your second trait as the area you flow to the quickest and with the most ease. For me, I am extremely outgoing (I am what we refer to as a double-outgoing blend). However, while I lean more toward being task-oriented, I can quickly flow between task or people orientation, almost interchangeably. It's about as quick as flipping a light switch.

Because of this, when I know I need to communicate with someone who is Supportive, I make a conscious effort to "shift" myself into my secondary trait, which puts me into a people-oriented mode. While this is not my "native" language, it is one I do operate in fluently. This allows me to focus on being in a people-oriented mode, which lets me find commonality with those in my lowest style as well.

Knowing that my primary style is the smallest percentage of the population, and the style I am the lowest in is the highest, this tactic has been more helpful to me personally and professionally through the years than just about any other.

I feel the need to make one more important note about our secondary styles, just to ensure there is no confusion. I mentioned in the chapters addressing each style that we can often find ourselves reverting to our secondary styles "out-of-control" during states of high stress. While that is totally true, I don't want you to think that is the only way we go there. Consider this—my secondary style is the one I understand the most besides my primary style. In my case, both of my top two traits literally chart in the identical place on a graph. So I can literally "flow" between both modes effortlessly.

If you find that you have two traits that both constantly seem to fit you, it may simply be that you are very high in both traits and that they would plot very close together on a personality graph. Remember, we are all a unique blend.

How the Gospels Represented All Four Styles

"For God is not the author of confusion *but of peace,*
as in all the churches of the saints" (I Corinthians 14:33, NKJV).

In each of the Gospel accounts, we are given a glimpse into the different ways in which the personality of Jesus was presented. We also know that because God is a God of order, nothing is done by chance. So, when we see things laid out for us in a way in which we never would have expected, we can rest assured knowing that He orchestrated it all from the very beginning.

I often wondered why the Gospel was given in four different accounts. Maybe, just maybe, it was because God (in His infinite wisdom) wanted to ensure that everything was shared in a way that would connect with anyone, regardless of how they were God-Wired.

In the fourth chapter of Revelation, we are given a glimpse of the throne. In that depiction, we see four creatures which all represent the four faces of redemption. As we will see, all four are a reflection of Jesus.

"Before the throne there was a sea of glass, like crystal. And in the midst of the throne, and around the throne, were four living creatures full of eyes in front and in back. The first living creature was like a lion, the second living creature like a calf, the third living creature had a face like a man, and the fourth living creature was like a flying eagle" (Revelation 4:6–7, NKJV).

Stick with me here. When you see it, it will make complete sense. Each of the creatures represented a perspective of the Gospel. The lion represented Jesus as the Messiah. In other words, it was His legal right to redeem mankind. The calf (many translations use the term ox) represented Jesus as the sacrifice for mankind. The man represented Jesus as the full man that He was. This was crucial because man gave up his place in the garden when Adam sinned. Only a man could legally take it back. Last, the eagle represented the full deity of Jesus. Because He was fully God in the flesh.

Each of the Gospel accounts focused heavily on one of the portrayals. If I were to relate the Gospel accounts to the DISC model, it would be written in reverse. They are actually laid out in CSID order. Knowing how He God-Wired humanity, it makes perfect sense.

In Matthew, Jesus was introduced as the Messiah. Before anything else could occur, it had to be very clear that He fulfilled the legal requirements laid out in the Old Covenant to claim the position as Messiah. He was introduced here as the "Lion of the tribe of Judah." The lion was the first creature listed in order in Revelation 4.

In Mark, Jesus was introduced as our sacrifice. Mark focused on portraying Jesus as the strong, yet humble servant who was the sacrificial lamb that would pay for our sins. Interesting, because the calf (sacrifice) was the second creature listed in order in Revelation 4.

In Luke, Jesus was introduced as the man that He was. Since man had given away his position with God, it would require a man to take that position back. That was why Jesus had to operate as a man under the Abrahamic covenant. He had to do what no man had done before. He had to live a sinless life to be able to reclaim what was once ours. The face of man was the third creature listed in order in Revelation 4.

Finally, in John, Jesus was introduced as the God He was. The deity of Jesus was literally the focus from the very first verse of John.

"In the beginning was the Word, and the Word was with God, and the Word was God. He was in the beginning with God. All things were made through Him, and without Him nothing was made that was made. In Him was life, and the life was the light of men. And the light shines in the darkness, and the darkness did not comprehend it" (John 1:1–5, NKJV).

Make no mistake about it. God didn't just send "someone" to sacrifice for us. He literally sent His most prized possession. Hopefully, that just goes to show you how much He loves YOU and thinks of YOU. But back to the point, the eagle was the fourth creature listed in order in Revelation 4.

Just as we have to love God with all of our heart, soul, mind, and strength, He had to show up fully expressing each category as well in order to lead by example. He did that (and then some) by showing up in all four perspectives.

I find it interesting that God addressed the legal and servant aspects to us first. These are essentially the C and S traits. Since roughly sixty percent of the population is Reserved, He spoke to us in our Reserved language first. In other words, connect with the most people immediately. Once we start to see it, we can't help but notice it more and more. There really is a pattern at work here.

Then He spoke to us, addressing His humanity and deity, speaking to our Outgoing natures. These are essentially the I and D traits. Of course, God is history's greatest "Master Communicator." He made us all. He God-Wired each of us. He understands exactly how we tick and knows how to communicate in a way to connect with us at the highest level.

In DISC, we see Him like this. The D trait represents His deity, which is portrayed by the eagle. The I trait represents His humanity, which is portrayed by the face of man. The S trait represents his sacrifice, which is portrayed by the calf (or ox). The C trait represents the legality of His claim, which is represented by the lion.

I love to summarize the Gospel message in this one statement. If He showed this much painstaking attention to detail in His plan to reconcile His relationship with you, then how much more does He need to do to show you how much He loves and values YOU? And if He loves and values you that much (which He does), then you should fully appreciate the way He God-Wired you. Whatever primary trait you have—if you haven't picked up on this already (multiple times, I hope)—you have an amazing personality style!

God (D) became man (I). He suffered and sacrificed Himself (S) to meet the requirements (C) of the Law.

PART III

Connecting
with Others

INTRO TO PART III

Look at you! You made it through Part Two. Congratulations! You should now have a solid understanding of who you are, as well as a deeper appreciation for those other temperaments that may not be like you at all.

For retention's sake, let's briefly review:

> **I** types are **inspiring**, **influencing**, **interesting** people, who are genuinely **interested** in other people. They are <u>fun</u> and <u>recognition</u>-oriented.

> **S** types are **supportive**, **sweet**, **servant-hearted**, **sentimental** people who, although **shy**, love to **serve** others. They are naturally the **sweetest** people in the world and are <u>harmony</u>-oriented.

> **C** types are **cautious**, **careful**, **compliance-wanting** people who want things done **correctly** the first time. They are **conscientious**, **consistent** people who are <u>excellence</u>-oriented.

> **D** types are **driven**, **dynamic**, **determined** people who thrive on **doing**, succeeding, winning, **dreaming**, and making things happen. They are **directors** who are <u>results</u>-oriented.

I love how all of these different temperaments have their own desires and wishes and how they react to different scenarios. Here are a couple related to driving to laugh at:

While driving down the road, someone pulls in front of you—here's how the different styles might react:

The I type might think, *Oh my gosh! They're driving fast! I'll bet they're having fun in that car. I wonder what music they're listening to? I'll bet if we rode together, we'd be best friends!*

The S type might think, *I'll slow down for them. They have somewhere else to be that's probably very important. I hope they're okay.*

The C type might think, *You know they didn't signal before they moved. That's an improper lane change. They're also exceeding the speed limit by at least 10 mph. Were they wearing their seat belt?*

The D type might think, *Okay, buddy. You were in a hurry to get in front of me. You'd better* stay *that way.* Then they're looking for an opportunity to get around them so they can be in front again.

Here's another scenario to consider:

You get into your car and plug the directions into your phone. The directions pop up and you look at them.

The I type might think, *The directions are in and I'm ready to go!* If nobody is in the car with them, they'd immediately call someone to talk to them. If someone is in the car, they immediately start telling them an incredible story that the person will find funny and engaging. In the process of the storytelling on the phone or in person, they will have completely missed their first and second turn. The number one thing their phone continually tells them is "Recalculating," and it doesn't bother them a bit!

The S type might think, *I just love my GPS on my phone. It's such a sweet, calming voice. Even when I mess up, it never raises its voice at me. It just calmly says, "recalculating" and helps me get to my destination. It's so sweet.*

The C type might think, *Look at that route. It's completely wrong! Who programmed this thing? There's no way this is right. Why in the world did they even consider going down this road? You could have saved three minutes if you'd have stayed on Main Street. Next time, call me and let me program this thing.*

The D type looks at one thing and one thing alone: the estimated arrival time. That time represents a direct challenge to everything a D stands for. They know they're going to beat that time and conquer the GPS challenge.

Isn't it funny how the different temperaments relate to the same situation? That's part of how we're all God-Wired differently. As you've read through the previous chapters and these two examples, you probably had moments where you smiled and said, "Yep. That's one hundred percent me!" Or you might've just nodded and said, "That's pretty close. Not exactly me, but close." Or . . . you had moments where you said, "That's not me at all, but I know exactly who that is just like."

It's easy to look at the descriptions and see who we are and who we aren't. We love that part. In fact, it comes naturally. Think about it this way. When you're in a group photo with ten or more people (or sometimes less), what is the determining factor that tells you whether it's a "good" photo or not? Be honest!

Most of us find ourselves in the photo first, then look at our facial expression, pose, and hair; and if we like how we look, then we deem it a "good photo," but—do we actually spend that same amount of time and use that same criterion with everyone else in the photo? Of course we don't. We typically focus on ourselves. It's just human nature.

This next part is about connecting with the other temperaments that not only aren't like us, but in many cases are the exact opposite of us.

It's easy to see how we are, but how do we do in seeing others the way they are?

Jesus gave us two commandments in Mark 12:29–31 (it's technically three):

> *"The first of all the commandments is: 'Hear, O Israel, the Lord our God, the Lord is one. And you shall love the Lord your God with all your heart, with all your soul, with all your mind, and with all your strength.' This is the first commandment. And the second, like it, is this: 'You shall love your neighbor as yourself.' There is no other commandment greater than these."*

The two parts of the second commandment Jesus told us are about loving our *neighbor* and about loving *ourselves*.

Let's deal with both.

Until we realize and begin to appreciate the temperament that we were God-Wired with, and that we're just fine with it, we won't be able to love ourselves properly. We need to celebrate our unique giftedness. You didn't hear the Apostle Paul complaining that he couldn't fish like Simon Peter. You didn't hear him complaining that he should be able to speak more like Peter. Peter spoke to large crowds. Paul was more of a small group guy. Some theologians have theorized that Paul actually suffered from a form of stage fright. You don't hear Peter complaining that he couldn't write as eloquently as Paul. The point is, they both had their own gifts and abilities. Peter was a great connector with people in crowds. Paul was a great leader in difficult situations. The Body of Christ required <u>both</u> gifts and temperaments to be in operation to succeed.

But what about connecting with the people who aren't like us? That's where "loving our neighbor" comes into the picture.

When we attempt to see things from their perspective before our own, we're loving our neighbor.

When we attempt to speak their temperamental language before we speak our own that we're more familiar with, we're loving our neighbor.

To paraphrase St. Francis of Assisi, when we seek to understand before being understood, we're loving our neighbor.

When I insist on only using <u>my</u> language and expect everyone to adapt to me, I am only loving myself. Imagine, for a moment, going to another country where your native language isn't spoken, and insisting everyone speak your language? Think for a second how incredibly inconsiderate that would be. Imagine someone from another country who did not speak your language coming to your country and insisting you speak their language. Not only would it be rude, but it would also be ridiculous!

And yet, we do it every day in our temperamental languages. We insist others adapt to us rather than learning each other's languages and speaking them for others' benefit.

When I am using their language and attempting to understand them first, I am loving them as I love myself.

Here's a hard truth to accept when understanding others who aren't like us. *What causes us pleasure can actually, and often does, cause them pain.*

Yes. It actually hurts them. What do I mean?

An I personality thrives on having fun. They love laughter and lots of interaction. Put a C personality in that same scenario, and it can be painful for them. Let's take the reverse. Put an I personality in an atmosphere where everyone has their nose to the grindstone, individually hammering out details to perform a job effectively and to absolute perfection with little to no interaction, and the group is thriving. An I personality would consider that atmosphere and lack of interaction to be stifling and . . . painful.

Where part two was all about understanding who we are, how we're wired, as well as comprehending the other temperaments, part three is going to be about *connecting* with each other.

I can read an instruction manual for how to assemble something...

Okay, let's be real here—I'm a D temperament—this scenario of reading an entire assembly manual has never actually happened to me, which is why I normally have unnecessary parts left over after my assembly, but . . . I know people who do read the instructions and use every part. Sorry—chased that squirrel—back to the book.

I can read an instruction manual for how to assemble something, but that doesn't mean I can actually do it; and it definitely doesn't mean it's automatically put together because I read a manual. I must put into practice the information I've been given to connect the right pieces for it to be what it's supposed to be. The same is true here.

The chapters in this third part will consist of several sections to help solidify how to connect with others, and those sections are called pain points, misperception points, desires, and connection points...

Pain points: When I travel to another country, I almost invariably find out the social faux pas I could potentially commit to avoid unnecessary embarrassment. For instance—being in the Middle East and being told to relax and "make yourself at home," then putting your feet up on a chair to relax. (I will not confirm nor deny I did this— you figure it out.) And then having to apologize for being an ignorant, rude American who didn't realize that showing the bottom of the soles of your feet to people is one of the most derisive things a person can do in that culture (imagine flipping the bird to someone in America—only worse).

We're going to explore the pain points for each personality style that we might not even think about. Consider this, too, that as you view these pain points, you may instantly think, *That's ridiculous! Who in their right mind could be offended by that?* But remember, this isn't your personality or your culture. It's theirs! Whether you understand it or not, it's our job to love others from their perspective and meet them where they are, and not show the soles of our feet accidentally! Yeah, it's still painful when I think about that one.

Misperception Points. Remember us talking about intent? It's easy to judge someone else's intent based on our biases. But that's the worst thing we can do if we want to connect with them! I'm convinced the largest gap in communication is the gap between what we're positive we know and what actually is true. We have to set aside what we think we know and actually give everyone the same benefit of good intentions that we give ourselves. Let's be clear; we are **not saying this is how you are!** It is simply how others can misjudge you. It's what we all have to overcome, and each temperament has these misperceptions. Don't consider it a label, merely a warning, or even a "cheat sheet" as to how you can overcome the way others may misunderstand you.

Desires: This is what each temperament is looking for. It was Zig Ziglar who said, *"You can have everything you want in life if you'll just help others get what they want."* That's not manipulation. That's simply adding value to others in the way they value and desire. This section will tell the basic wants and desires for that particular personality style. When you know what someone wants, it's also like having an answer key to a complicated test. It gives you a distinct advantage so you can connect with them.

Connection Points: This section will tell you ways your particular style can connect with this personality style. It will give you specific examples as well as some ideas to move you in the right direction. We'll also tell you how to deal with each personality style when they're out of control.

Finally, we'll recap to summarize that personality style and remind you again of the pain points, misperception points, desires, and connection points in a chart form so you can use it as a reference when you need it.

One final thought that we've touched on but not specifically said: Never, ever use any of this information to attempt to manipulate someone. That's wrong one hundred percent of the time. The purpose of studying these traits is to connect with others. Manipulation is used to get your own way. Connection is used to understand someone else and create a relationship that has mutual value.

Having said all of this—are you ready?

Let's jump into Part THREE!

8

CONNECTING WITH THE HEART

Al Denson is one of the best connectors I've ever known. Those who have been around contemporary Christian music for a while may recognize his name as the writer of "Will You Be the One?" and "Take Me to the Cross." Denson is also the compiler of the *Youth Worship Chorus Book* used by many churches in the early '90s.

He is an off-the-scale "I" personality style whose love for people is as genuine as it is contagious. He is fun. He is funny. Spend your day with Al and you will laugh as hard as you ever have; and years later, you'll remember that day as one of your best.

We were in Russia a few years ago touring an upscale museum. By upscale, I mean there were Rembrandts and a da Vinci painting in this museum. <u>BIG TIME</u> nice! Al decided to stay back in the lobby, and the rest of us took the nearly two-hour tour through some of the most spectacular works of art anybody has ever seen.

When we returned to the lobby, Al was behind the information desk, passing out the informational brochures to tourists. I couldn't believe what I was seeing. He was smiling at all of them, and they smiled back. When the person who was actually supposed to be working the desk returned with a surprised look on their face, Al smiled at them and said something; and then ... the lady who was returning to work smiled at him, thanked him, and then *hugged him*. That's right. If you know anything about the Russian people, you <u>know</u> how rare this is.

Anybody else would've ended up in a Russian prison, but not Al. He is a master of connecting. To be with Al around eating time means two things: One, you're going to have one of the best meals of your life; and two, you're going to watch a master at work in making complete strangers feel as if he is their new best friend.

His family calls it "ADM" ("Al Denson Magic"). He will walk into the room and get to know complete strangers. I've even seen him buy their meals. He'll end up knowing details about each person because he is genuinely interested in them. The funny part is, he may not remember their names, but he'll remember all sorts of details about them that others would instantly forget. The people he encounters truly feel he is one of their best friends, even though they have just met.

There have been times I've been with him, and he recommends a restaurant "he just ate at last week and the food is phenomenal." So, we go, and when we walk in the door, it's like I'm with Norm at Cheers. The hostesses and managers all yell out, "Al!" as if they've known him all their lives.

I asked him once at a place in Dallas, when a manager came to our table and talked to us for about fifteen minutes, "How many times have you been to this place?" Al flatly replied, "Once." To anybody else, you'd have thought they had known each other for ten years.

Al connects to people's hearts because his huge heart is opened to them.

There are some of you reading this right now, however, for whom the entire scenario I've just described either stresses you out, turns you off, or makes you feel like the entire thing is contrived. I can assure you from having witnessed years of Al, it isn't contrived. It's real.

But how do you connect with an I when everything I've just described sounds foreign and maybe even painful for you?

Let's talk about some pain points for an I:

Pain Points:

1. The thing that causes the most heartache for those who connect with their hearts is the feeling that a person

doesn't like them. If someone verbalizes dislike for an I, it's even worse.

On one occasion, when Al and I were in Jerusalem with a large group waiting to eat at a restaurant, he was doing his connection thing, but one guy basically told him, "I don't want to talk. Please leave me alone."

I wouldn't dream of judging the intent of this man. Maybe he was dealing with something deep inside that none of us knew about and just wanted to be alone. Who knows? But I do know that was a pain point for Al. Not simply because of the rejection, but because of Al's desire to bring joy and happiness and a smile to everyone he meets.

2. Another pain point would be a stoic situation where nobody is smiling or having fun. I was in a very serious meeting, and during a particularly contentious part, an I in the meeting blurted out, "I think we need to watch something funny. We need to laugh in here."

Two of the C styles in the room rolled their eyes immediately. I (in my D style) said, "I think we need to get through this so we can go on with our day," to which the I instantly shot back, "I think you need to learn to have a little fun in your life."

We were there to get a job done, but I was inadvertently causing pain to the I in the room by the constant barrage of details and work without injecting any humor or fun into the situation.

3. A third pain point would be an unwillingness to talk or verbalize. I styles thrive on talking. They work out many of their issues through verbalization, and they expect the same out of you. So, when you look at an I who says, "How are you doing?" and refuse to answer or worse yet, even ignore them, you're causing them pain. Maybe even emotional trauma.

4. A fourth pain point would be ignoring an I. This is one of the worst things you can do to them. It's one thing to feel someone doesn't like them, but it's much worse to feel that they matter so little to someone that they don't even acknowledge their presence or contributions. I styles love recognition. Ignoring someone is the opposite of recognizing them.

5. A fifth pain point would be public humiliation. As you'll see in a minute, I personality styles thrive on public recognition. Any kind of public humiliation is devastating for them.

6. A sixth pain point is a lack of emotional involvement or awareness. I styles will filter everything through their emotions, so if you filter it all through logic, you will automatically be on two different pages. If you're not an emotional person by nature, connecting with an I will always be a stretch, but . . . it *can* be done.

Misperception Points:

As you read these, please keep in mind that we are *not* saying this is how anyone actually is. We're simply saying this could be how others misperceive you.

1. I personality styles can be seen as silly. Their desire to share humor with others can give the impression to certain personality styles that they are not to be taken seriously or are generally silly people.

2. They can also be seen as overly emotional. Since their emotions drive so much of what they do, they can be perceived as too emotional to reason with.

3. They can be seen as trying too hard to be liked. They may even jump into conversations they know nothing about or take over conversations to tell their amazing story, all the while not realizing that it comes across as them trying too hard to make everyone laugh or make everyone like them.

4. Because of their desire to tell stories, engage people, and have fun, they can be viewed as unfocused or even borderline ADD. (Remember Doug in the movie, *Up*?— "Squirrel!")

Desires:

An I personality style is looking for:

-   Recognition (Publicly! They like being the center of attention.)

-   Approval ("I like you!")

-   Fun ("Let's do it the FUN way!" "Can we make this a game?")

-   Humor (They like to laugh, but they enjoy making others laugh more, as long as it isn't at their expense.)

-   Interaction with others (They thrive on interacting with other people and derive energy from being around others.)

-   Lots of activity (They're on the run all the time, as long as it's fun.)

Connection Points:

How do you connect with an I? The good news is, it's pretty simple.

1. Consider approaching them in a way that connects. The simplest way is something that comes naturally to most people: Ask, "How are you doing today?" Then *let them talk*. They may not take a breath for the next twenty minutes; but they *need* to talk, and they *need* you to listen. Be interested in them. Remember, I types are **interesting** people.

    I know—I hear you: "But what if I don't have that kind of time?" My best suggestion is, when talking to an I—plan accordingly. Make that time.

2. SMILE. I have an issue with my face. My kids told me about it. It has initials which stand for something not nice, so I'm not going to print it here, but some of you know what I'm talking about. My natural look when I'm listening intently or concentrating on something is to frown with my eyebrows furrowed—so much so that people would ask me, "Ken—are you Okay? Why are you mad?" I wasn't mad. I was simply focused.

    This was especially noticeable to the I types in my life. They thought I was perpetually mad, and I really wasn't. I had to make a change. I had to intentionally make myself smile—especially when I was around I type people. I just made it a point to smile at them.

    Smiling may not be a natural state for you either, but if you want to connect with an I, you need to do it. If you can muster a laugh at their stories or jokes, too, that's a huge plus. I'm not suggesting that you act like something you're not, but at the very least, try to allow yourself to enjoy their story and find some humor in it that elicits something on your face besides a frown!

3. Tell them something you like about them personally. They like to be liked. If this occurs in front of others, it will produce an even better result. That public recognition is a big deal to them.

4. If you're a task-oriented person, try to incorporate a little fun into the productivity. An I will respond much better to making a game out of being productive than they will by asking them to be more serious.

5. If you don't feel you can make it fun, at the very least be positive. An I type will not like negativity. They thrive on positivity.

6. Look for the I personality's strength zone. They're natural connectors with people. They're the ones you want connecting with your people. Doing this gives them the chance to shine, which they love to do.

Jim Biggs is a faithful member of my church. Most every Sunday, he spends his time walking around the lobby, greeting people, smiling, laughing, joking, and . . . connecting. He's always quick with a smile and a joke. He makes people feel welcome. He is great with names. He's friendly. Most people love him.

Our church had the reputation of being one of the most unfriendly churches in our city. When I began working with our hospitality, I did DISC assessments on them. Guess which personality style we were missing in our hospitality group? Yup. We only had one I—Jim Biggs. He was the friendly face. Every other person was a task-side person, plus a couple of S styles who were naturally shy.

In the next three months, I repurposed some of the people into other more task-oriented roles, and I asked Jim to help me recruit people who were more like him. The next year, our church became known as one of the friendliest places in our city, and this past year, we placed second in the city's "Best of the Best" places to worship.

But how did Jim and I recruit them? We told them how much FUN it would be for them to talk to new people and make some new friends. We also recognized our hospitality people from the pulpit. I mean, we stood them up and clapped for them. Can you say public recognition?

Putting those friendly, fun, smiling faces around the front of our building made a huge difference. I needed those I types in their places, doing what they do best: CONNECTING.

Let's review:

I personality styles like to be liked. They thrive on public recognition. They love to laugh and tell stories. They have lots of best friends and would love to add you as one of them. They appreciate being included in many social activities.

They don't like any type of public criticism or humiliation. It crushes them to hear the words, "I don't like you!" They don't like being left out of anything.

Phrases an I personality loves to hear:

"I really like you!"

"You're fun!"

"Tell me that story you told me the other day."

"Can we have lunch?"

"Do you want to hang out with us?"

"How are you doing?" (Then really let them tell you!)

"Tell me about your day."

"Do you want to stand up and give our report in front of everybody?"

"Can you tell us how we can be more friendly and connect with more people?"

Tell them a story about yourself. If it's humorous, all the better. However—be ready for them to tell you their story immediately afterward and for it to be bigger and better than yours. You'll get major bonus points for listening intently to that story and being interested in it.

And the ultimate:

"Can we be friends?"

I personality styles connect with their heart. If you're going to connect with them, you have to meet them at <u>their</u> heart too.

How do you handle an I personality style that is out of control? An I pushed out of control generally becomes illogical. This means they are capable of doing anything. Remember that I types are very emotional people who are driven by their feelings. When pushed out of control, emotions take over, and appealing to their logic is pretty much useless. It's best to reinforce to them that you truly like them and let their emotional state subside.

When they "come down" from their emotional peaks, they will be more likely to listen to logic and reason. However—it's important that you help them see how doing what you ask will not only keep them from looking bad (which they despise!), but it will also cause others to have more fun; and it could shine a positive spotlight on them. Remember, I types like positive recognition. Your approach with I types must always be seasoned with positive affirmations and even some fun and levity.

Finally, it's important to note that the heart is one of the main ways we connect with God, especially with reference to our salvation.

"That if you confess with your mouth Jesus as Lord and believe in your heart God has raised Him from the dead, you shall be saved. For with the heart one believes unto righteousness, and with the mouth confession is made unto salvation" (Romans 10:9–10, NKJV).

God values how we believe in our hearts, and we should value the hearts of other people too.

Style Tips to connect with an I:

If you're a D:

- You and the I type are both outgoing, so you have a potential connection in that you both have no trouble expressing yourself. The conflict can occur when you're talking over each other and both temperaments tend to interrupt. Make a concerted effort to listen and to hear them out before talking about what you want. This will be the most difficult part for you.

- You're very task-oriented and very bottom line. An I could perceive that as being blunt or downright rude. Show a genuine interest in them before you try to ask for anything you want.

- Smile! It may not come naturally to you, but do it anyway. That smile will go a long way in connecting with an I.

- Say what you want in a pleasant and even fun manner. I types are sensitive people and can personalize something that you didn't at all mean personally. Remember, with them, it's not what you say, it's *how* you say it!

- Go ahead and get over the fact that this encounter will be longer than you want it to be. There will be stories told and things shared that have zero to do with what you're wanting, but if you truly want to connect with them, you're going to have to step through their territory first to get to your goal later.

- Consider sharing a funny story or even a joke (an appropriate one) you've heard. Sharing a laugh is an instant way of connecting with an I. Be ready for them to share their joke/story (or stories) after you do. This is all part of the connection process with them.

- If, by chance, the person says something that sets in a wrong way with you, do *not* respond. Chances are good they didn't realize it and didn't mean it. Ignore it and go on.

If you're an I:

- Hey! Hey! PARTY TIME! You both love to have fun. You both love to laugh. You both love to tell stories. You both love to smile. Enjoy it!

- Remember *why* you're there. If there is a task to be performed, don't become so social that you forget the reason you're together.

- If there isn't a task to be performed—and the connection is purely social—party on, Garth!

- The potential for conflict here only exists if there is a division over who will get the spotlight for an activity. My suggestion? Get two spotlights. You're both stars! Go shine!

- Let's be honest—connecting with another I will not be a problem. It's the party with your best friend that doesn't end!

If you're an S:

- You and the I type already share a love for people, so it's much easier to connect with them since you both care deeply for people.

- Since you don't like to talk nearly as much as they do, ask them questions. If you get to the end of the conversation and they've talked about ninety percent of the time, you'll likely be considered their new best friend as well as the best conversationalist they've ever known.

- Smile and laugh with them. You genuinely love people. Let them know by your eye contact, your attentiveness, and, most of all, your *responses* (visually and verbally!) that you're enjoying the conversation.

- You're a great, friendly person. Be *you*. They'll love you for it.

- At the end, let them know that talking to them was a lot of fun and you're looking forward to the next conversation.

- If you notice something they've said or done that you can positively reinforce, do it! Remember that they love to be recognized and affirmed.

If you're a C:

- Realize that you and the I types are polar opposites. This means as a C, out of all the temperaments, you and the I types have the least in common.

- A *smile* will go way further than your details. An I personality type isn't interested in details, and they don't connect with details. They connect with fun, or, as we like to say it, often, people ARE their details.

- Try to find a humorous story or a joke you can share with them. It's not necessarily in your primary nature, but it's worth it if it helps you accomplish your task with excellence.

- Accept that the encounter will be longer than you want, and it might contain some exaggeration of the facts. (That's not lying, by the way. I types tend to speak in exaggerated superlatives. It's just part of their nature.) Yes, it will definitely be longer than you planned for it to be. They're talkers! As a C, you love "process." Just consider that this is *their* process. While it is different from yours, accepting the need to follow this process is what you need to do if you want to connect with them.

- You have a deep need to be thorough and share every detail. It's worth mentioning again: an I will not connect to your details. As unfathomable as that may be, they aren't the least bit interested in them. They're not detail-oriented (which probably drives you up a wall). They are FUN oriented. They are recognition-oriented (which you probably don't care about either).

- If there is an accomplishment that they've done that you can recognize or affirm, *do it*. It'll help you connect quicker.

- If an I type says something you know to be incorrect, don't correct them. Just let them talk. Nobody likes being corrected, and an I personality could take your correction as a personal attack. Remember, you're not there to correct; you're there to *connect*!

9

CONNECTING WITH THE SOUL

The ocean is deep . . . very deep. Scientists tell us that if you were to shave off all the land on every continent and island of the world, and fill up the ocean's deepest parts, the entire earth would still be covered with water two miles deep.[3]

An S personality is very much the same way. They're normally way deeper than we give them credit for. Sometimes, their shy demeanor can make you think it isn't there, but never doubt it. It's there.

An S personality has clearly definable pain points.

Pain Points:

1. Anything that is loud. You can say something that is complimentary or nice to an S, and it'll still be bad for them if it's spoken in a loud tone. They dislike being around people who are loud or boisterous and can be stressed out by them.

2. Confrontation. This is almost impossible for an S to do. It takes everything in them to confront anyone, and they'll do nearly anything to avoid it at all costs. They'll even avoid it to their own demise. Yes, they'd rather get sick to the point of death than be forced to confront someone.

3. Misunderstandings. This is closely related to confrontation. They want peace on their borders, and

---

[3] https://www.youtube.com/watch?v=GE-lAftuQgc&ab_channel=RealLifeLore

misunderstandings cause ripples in their pond that can take months or even years to level out.

4. Insensitivity. This style is the most sensitive of all the styles. They just may not verbalize it like others would. But remember that deep ocean: just because you can't see it, doesn't mean it isn't there.

5. Public recognition or public speaking. This is akin to confrontation for them. They don't want to stand up and be seen in any way, shape, or form. It has been said the number one fear is public speaking. The number two fear is death. Comedian Jerry Seinfeld observed, "That means if you were at a funeral, you would rather be the one in the casket than the one delivering the eulogy!" S types can relate to this statement.

6. Closely related to the previous one, they don't like surprises. An I type would thrive with a surprise party. They'd love the recognition and the human interaction. An S would die in that atmosphere. They would feel the weight of a spotlight that they never wanted or desired. Never surprise an S!

7. Change. Of all the personality styles, the S is the most resistant to change. They enjoy status quo. I guarantee you, "If it ain't broke, don't fix it" was spoken by an S the first time! Before you misunderstand this need in them, it is important to understand why this is a big deal. To an S, change implies risk. In their mind, risk automatically carries with it a chance that the change could potentially cause others hurt or stress.

8. Sarcasm—Pay attention, D and I types! This may seem funny to you, but it isn't to an S. They take it to heart and will shut you down. Very similar to the way a turtle thumped on its shell retreats, so will an S do to you if you're sarcastic with them. Try to force a turtle to come back out of a shell and let me know how that works for you. It's not going to happen. They'll come back out

when they're good and ready. A good rule of thumb: when communicating with a turtle, it's best not to thump the shell at all.

9. Conflict. Let's be clear on this—I don't mean conflict with them, although that would be a part of it, as seen previously. I mean conflict around them . . . even if *you* don't view it as conflict!

My primary type is a D personality. I had another D in my office, and we were discussing (or you might call it having some "intense fellowship") an issue and doing what Ds do: raising our voices, talking with our hands, standing up, sitting down, being animated. Hey— that's just normal for us. We weren't mad.

My office door was shut and my assistant, Kaye (an S!), was sitting at her desk the entire time. After about forty-five minutes of us "fellowshipping," the other D left. Now bear in mind—we were fine. All good. No problems. No issues. No animus. No nothing.

When I walked out to Kaye's office, she was clearly rattled. Even upset. Not one thing we talked about had *anything* to do with her, but her being close to the conflict stressed her out; and yes—it caused her pain. I ended up sending her home early that day, and I learned my lesson. If I must have an intense conversation, it's best to do that outside of the proximity of Kaye or any other S type in my life.

Misperception Points:

Please keep in mind as you read these that we are *not* saying this is how anyone actually is. We're simply saying this is how you could be misperceived by others.

1. S personalities can be seen as snobs. Now I know every S that read that just cringed and thought—I've never been a snob! A snob thinks they're better than others, and I've never thought that. And you're right. You've never thought that way.

2. But consider that some people may *mistakenly* think you are acting like a snob because of your shyness and lack of initiative for talking to people. They may mistakenly think that you don't engage in conversation for a reason besides the fact that you just don't initiate discussions. I get it! You're waiting for someone to talk to you, and then you're happy to engage. But it's important to know that initially, you can be misperceived and misjudged if you don't at least smile or say "hi."

3. S personalities can be seen as rebellious to authority. Okay—now hold on! That's two for two! Again—I get it! You're NOT! But stay with me for a moment and ask yourself this question: Do you enjoy change?

4. When you resist change, it can be misconstrued as resisting authority. The truth is, those in authority likely didn't give you the prerequisite information and time to adapt to that change. However, it is a misperception that can be there.

5. S personalities can often be seen and treated as doormats. This comes from a simple word that can easily escape their vocabulary. That word is "no," which, by the way, is a complete sentence. An S is not a doormat, nor should they be treated that way, but they can easily be taken advantage of by people who are habitual users and takers. S types have to learn that saying "no" may actually *serve* someone and help them more than saying "yes."

Desires:

An S personality is looking for:

- Peace on their borders. They thrive in peaceful atmospheres.

- Predictability. As stated earlier, An S will not enjoy a changing atmosphere. They derive a sense of peace and security from knowing things will remain as predictable as they always have been.

- Opportunities to serve and help others. An S loves to serve the needs of others and feels great joy and satisfaction in doing so.

- Kindness and thoughtfulness in others. They enjoy being around others who are kind and gentle and sweet, like themselves. They respect people who value people before things or tasks.

- Thoughtful, private recognition. An S will want to be recognized and appreciated for their accomplishments, but not publicly. They prefer a private, face-to-face conversation or a handwritten card. Those things mean more to them than anything in public.

- Patience and understanding, not only with them, but with others too.

Connection Points:

1. Lower your voice tone. If you're naturally an intense or animated speaker, you'll need to pull things way back when speaking to an S, or they'll shut down and not hear you.

2. Consider their feelings and the feelings of other people in the room equally. S types respect leaders who consider the feelings of others before themselves.

3. Remember that change is not something they will embrace without a lot of time. An S is very similar to a 777 jet at an airport. It requires a long, long runway to build up enough speed for takeoff. That's how you approach change with an S. At first, you introduce the idea. They likely will barely acknowledge what you've said, but never doubt the stone you just threw in the deep ocean sank all the way to the bottom. They heard you. Then you must prepare them for how the change will serve other people and help everyone. And you must prepare them a long time prior to when you actually are

implementing the shifts. I'm not talking days or even weeks. I'm talking months, or possibly a year.

4. Think of the difference between a jet ski and a cruise ship. A jet ski can turn on a dime, throwing a huge rooster tail of water in the air and zooming off immediately in another direction. Personality styles like Ds and Is can navigate change this way. An S type cannot do this. They are like huge cruise ships. Spin the wheel of a large ship and it will start changing direction, but it's a very slow change and will take time. View change with S types in a cruise ship manner, not the jet ski way.

5. Help them understand how much you appreciate their servant heart and how you'll protect it. Chances are good that their natural desire to serve others has led to them being taken advantage of by many. Reassure them and *show them* that you're not one of them.

6. Let them know how much they're valued as a person. Find attributes about them you can appreciate that won't change (their honesty, their servant heart, their kindness, their generosity, etc.). Make sure this appreciation is done face-to-face or with a nice handwritten note. You could also give them a thoughtful gift. Remember, too—a thoughtful gift isn't necessarily an expensive one. Thoughtful means just that; there was some thought behind what you gave them, and the gift has a special meaning to them. I know one S type who keeps a rock on her desk because it has sentimental value for her. To others, it would just be a rock, but to her, it has a very special meaning.

7. IF there is any type of conflict, you *must* remember to affirm them, and affirm their value, and then address the conflict as lightly as possible. Remember that they truly want to serve and are natural people pleasers. They don't need a sledgehammer; they need velvet gloves.

8. This is the biggest one. Help them say "no" because they have so much trouble saying it themselves. They'll help others until they drown themselves. Sometimes, they have to be protected from themselves, and if you're in the position to do so, you'll earn their trust and respect if you do just that.

Veterinarians tell us that a horse can run and run and run until their heart explodes and they fall over dead. S personalities can be the same way. If you see this happening, and you have influence in that area, you should try to help and keep them from imploding.

Phrases an S personality loves to hear:

(Remember! These need to be spoken in a calmer, quieter, more soothing tone!)

"Having you around brings such peace to me and this place."

"Thank you for your kindness and sensitivity in this manner."

"You really helped me."

"Thank you for your service." (This one is best done face-to-face while maintaining eye contact.)

"I appreciate and value you for (insert an attribute about them as well as something they may have accomplished)."

"Your feelings about this are very important to me."

"Can you give me some ways we all could connect better as a team?" (Because S types are naturally good listeners, be ready for some major insights from them if they're willing to give them to you!)

"I have something I'm wanting to express to someone, but I'm concerned about how it could be perceived. Could you please help me word this in a way that is kind but still gets my point across in a sincere and genuine way?"

I've used the above phrase with my assistant Kaye after I've written letters that could be a bit confrontational. I would show them to her before I sent them. She immediately saw some things and gently told me, "Oh . . . I'm not sure I'd say it like that. What about this instead?" Her sensitive nature is a huge asset to me and helps balance my typically direct nature, and she has saved me some unnecessary misunderstandings and even heartaches.

And here's the biggest phrase you *must* be judicious in using with an S: "Would you be willing to help me with _____?" They will normally say yes unless it involves some sort of public speaking or confrontation, but if it's behind the scenes, they'll be all in. I say you need to be careful in asking because you need to be sure you're guarding their time and not letting them become overwhelmed!

How do you deal with an S out of control? Well—if the turtle shell has been thumped and they've shut down, the worst thing you can do is push. The more you push, the more they're going to retreat into their shell. If you push your agenda, you're not giving them one of their greatest desires: *peace*! The only thing you can do here is reinforce (calmly and gently!) that you value them and tell them that if/when they would like to talk to you, it would help you and the organization to do so. Given time, they'll normally come around, but it'll be on their timetable, not yours.

Style Tips for Connecting with an S:

If you're a D:

- Realize that you and the S are polar opposites. This means as a D, out of all the temperaments, you and the S type have the least in common.

- Your approach will be *everything* in this encounter. Chances are good they already have a preconceived notion that you are overbearing, demanding, and possibly rude. You have to overcome this with your facial expressions, body language, and the first words out of your mouth.

- Smile. Be kind, gentle, and pleasant in your demeanor.

- The first thing you say (in a very calm, non-intense, non-intimidating way!) should be something along the lines of how much you value and appreciate them.

- The next thing you should do is ask sincerely how they're doing and then listen intently to how they answer.

- Never, ever, ever be sarcastic with them. The moment you do, the conversation is over—regardless of how much you keep talking or attempt to backtrack, saying, "I was just joking."

- Never, ever, ever raise your voice to them. The moment you do, the conversation is over.

- Listen intently and sincerely and try to understand their feelings. For them, feelings are very real and extremely important. To simply dismiss them to get to your own goal will come across as insensitive, selfish, uncompassionate, and even unkind. Every one of those will be a huge roadblock to connecting with an S.

- Never confront them. They'll shut down.

- If you have anything negative to say, your conversation should be ninety-nine percent positive, and then somewhere in the middle, fit in the conflict part. Remember that their nature is to please and serve, but if you mishandle this part, you can damage them to the point they won't want to interact with you anymore.

If you're an I:

- You and the S share a love for people, and that will be your connection point. Talk about how you love people.

- Smile a lot and be kind. This should come naturally to you.

- Because of your tendency to talk and dominate a conversation with your incredibly fun and interesting stories and anecdotes, it will be easy to do all the talking. Resist this urge and let them do the talking.

- Realize that they'll likely be reluctant to talk at first, but ask them questions and then resist the urge to interrupt them with your own stories. Once you get an S personality talking, they'll open up.

- Acknowledge that the louder you get, the quieter they will get, and that's not a good thing when you're trying to connect with them. (Refer back to the metaphor of thumping a turtle on its shell.)

- Understand that silence with them is not always negative. They may simply be processing their emotions. Where you process emotions externally, they process them internally.

- Never, ever, ever be sarcastic with them. Even if *you* think it's funny. They will just find it to be unkind. S types thrive on being kind to others, even those they don't necessarily agree with.

- If you're upset at someone else, sharing that with an S will introduce conflict into the relationship, which can instantly cause them to shut down.

- If you're upset with them, wait until you calm down to say anything. If you can't address it calmly, don't address it at all. They're sensitive just like you are, but overly emotional interactions will lead to the turtle retreating into their shell.

If you're an S:

- This interaction is going to be one of few words and a lot of peaceful quiet times, which should be pleasing to you.

- Enjoy the calm, meaningful interactions and the deep connections.

- Write encouraging notes to each other and/or exchange meaningful, thoughtful gifts.

If you're a C:

- You're both reserved, so talking to each other may not come naturally. Then again, you're both able to appreciate the lack of meaningless small talk.

- S types are people-oriented, which means you'll need to be interested in them personally before you try to get to what you want.

- Ask them about themselves, family, friends, and/or travel and then genuinely listen to their answers. Be sincerely interested. This is helping you accomplish your tasks with excellence by allowing them to buy-in.

- S types love to finish tasks. You love details. Try not to overwhelm them with too many details. If you do, it can lead them to "analysis paralysis," where instead of going through the details and moving forward, they'll become overwhelmed and stop. They only need enough of the details to complete the task at hand.

- If you give them instructions, be sure and repeat them, slowly and calmly, with a smile on your face.

- Details are what *you* are there for. They're there to serve.

- Be conscious of your facial expression and smile often.

- Be kind. What you consider to be straight-forward facts could be misconstrued as robotic, cold, and even rude and unkind by them.

- Reinforce how you respect their steadiness and reliability. These are traits you both share.

- Be affirming. If you're going to give details, give them details about how wonderful of a job they're doing in serving the organization by bringing peace and stability.

The condition of our soul matters to God.

"Now may the God of peace Himself sanctify you completely; and may your whole spirit, soul, and body be preserved blameless *at the coming of our Lord Jesus Christ"* (I Thessalonians 5:23, NKJV).

God also wants our souls to prosper and be in good health:

"Beloved, I pray that you may prosper in all things and be in health, just as your soul prospers" (3 John 2, NKJV).

We should value the condition of our souls as well. That means we should value loving ourselves. But if we're truly going to love our neighbors as ourselves, we must value their souls too. Those S personalities are the souls of our organizations. We need to value them, listen to them, allow them to thrive in their service to us, protect them from being overwhelmed by saying "yes" too much, and provide peaceful atmospheres in which they can thrive.

If you can connect with an S, you will have found yourself the most wonderful, sweetest, loyal, and trusted friend you'll ever have for your entire life.

10

CONNECTING WITH THE MIND

James (not his real name) worked for a government agency. He was known by his colleagues as being aloof, disengaged, and disinterested in people. He spent nearly every day in his office with the door closed. When there was any kind of social gathering, he never came out, or if he did, it was for a specific purpose that didn't involve talking with people. When he had to deal with people, it was in short, one-to-two-sentence factual bursts that often never waited for a response or required one.

He was generally known as anti-social. When I say anti-social, I don't just mean he didn't want to be around people. I mean, he didn't *like* being around people. In fact, he would only spend time with others when his boss told him he had to do it. When he did go to the social gatherings or even meetings, he would sit as far away from everyone as possible and refused to even look in the direction of others. He would stare out of the window as if he were daydreaming . . . but he wasn't. He was listening to every detail.

While he was known for this type of behavior, he was also known for being a complete necessity in the organization because of his efficiency. The place couldn't run without him because of his meticulous attention to detail that kept the organization in compliance and made things run smoothly. He could calculate in an instant what it took other people weeks to do, and those others still wouldn't do it at the level of excellence at which he performed. He not only didn't require any recognition for his accomplishments, but he also didn't want it. On more than a few occasions, he expressed by his actions and attitude that he simply wanted to be left alone to do his job. Needless to say, James is an off-the-scale C temperament.

So, you can imagine what his reaction was when a weekend staff retreat was held for all the department heads, and he was required to attend. A day and a half at a retreat center interacting with people was pain for James. It was awkward from the get-go. I was the speaker for this retreat, and I was talking about what you've been reading about, with the obvious exception that it was in a corporate setting, so it wasn't faith based like this book.

James just sat there, staring off into the distance. I was warned that he was next to impossible to connect with. While I talked, he never once picked up his pen or took one note, and yet—I knew he was listening to me. He never smiled at a single joke. He never reacted to my comments about the other styles.

But when I got to the part about the C styles and how to connect with them, I made this statement: "The C styles are spending their lives trying to fix all the stuff that the rest of you are messing up, when if you would just listen to them and do it right the first time, everything would be great!"

Most everyone laughed, except James. His reaction surprised everyone in the room, including me. As soon as the phrase left my mouth, his hands shot up in the air like he had scored a touchdown; and he exclaimed in a loud voice, "Thank you very much for saying that! Finally! Somebody gets it!"

At the end of that session, he actually high-fived me. Some of the other leaders in that group commented afterward that it was the biggest reaction they had seen from him in years. It wasn't impossible to connect with James. You simply had to take the correct pathway, and that pathway was details, excellence, and quality work.

C styles connect through their mind, not their emotions. If we're going to connect with them, we must do the same thing.

Pain Points:

1.   Anything done in a sloppy, substandard manner. They cannot function in this type of environment for any extended period of time because a lack of excellence

causes them pain.

2. Lack of details! They will push back and ask more and more questions because they crave details. It is a must-have!

3. Being incorrect. As we said previously, I do *not* mean they're know-it-alls. I mean that doing something incorrectly that could have been done correctly had they been given the pertinent details causes them pain.

   Think of it this way: If you plug the wrong mathematical details into a calculator, you cannot expect the right answer. With a calculator, you simply go back and insert the right inputs—it's a computer that only kicks out what you put into it. With a C style, plugging in the wrong inputs and getting the wrong results isn't simply an "Oh well" moment for them. It represents a waste of time and a mistake that could have been avoided if someone (namely you!) had taken the time to consider all the details in the first place. C types know the value of time and despise wasting it. After all, most of them have their entire day planned out, and they don't want that time wasted.

4. Being forced into social interactions with no purpose. The number one question a C will ask you is, "Why are we doing this?" If no clear purpose is given, their time is far too valuable, and their plans are laid out too far in advance for them to waste it on meetings or activities that do not produce excellence, quality, and a clearly defined (in advance!) purpose.

5. Clutter and disorganized messes. A C style will not stay in a disorganized environment. If they are forced to stay there, they'll likely "fix it" the way they deem it should be done. Staying around clutter and disorganization is painful for them.

A quick point here: I'm not saying every C style has an immaculate desk. In fact, sometimes it's quite the opposite. But don't mistake what looks like a "mess" to you as a disorganized pile of clutter. I guarantee you the C person can put their hands on whatever they want on their desk at any time. What appears messy to others is actually a highly organized stack of papers for them, and if someone "cleans it up"—Yikes! Look out!

6. Overly emotional people. Pay attention my "I" friends! Overly emotional people are immediately met by C styles with suspicion because they assume logic isn't in play. A C style will not operate by how they feel. They will only operate by what they think. Being in emotional situations causes stress for a C-style person.

7. Liars. Dishonesty is a deal breaker and is very difficult to overcome with a C style. Always tell them the truth. Do not exaggerate. Be exact in your phrasing.

8. Asking for an immediate answer before they've had a chance to research something. As mentioned in point three above, they'd rather be anything than incorrect. An immediate answer could be the wrong answer. C types need time to process and research. It's their nature to be this way. When asked for an immediate answer, expect them to ask for more time, rather than give you an incomplete answer that has not been properly researched.

Misperception Points:

Please keep in mind as you read these that we are *not* saying this is how anyone actually is. We're simply saying this is how you could be misperceived by others.

1. C styles can be seen as unemotional robots. In *Star Trek* terms, think Spock or Data. This can be intimidating and off-putting for people.

2. Because C styles are not driven by emotions but instead by logic, they can be seen as uncaring or unsympathetic to the needs of others. The way they like to do their work alone without interaction can also contribute to this misperception. They're not. They show they care by their attention to detail and excellent work.

3. Know-It-Alls. C styles are well studied and well researched. They are a wealth of knowledge. But sharing that knowledge with everyone (even when the person sharing the knowledge is wrong!) can make a C seem like an arrogant know-it-all.

4. Mean. I know! You're not! But it is a common misperception because of the lack of any emotional responsiveness or smiling.

Desires:

A C style is looking for:

- A functionally excellent organization.

- Quality work and quality answers.

- Clear information and detailed instructions.

- Information that tells them WHY they're doing what they're being asked to do.

- One hundred percent honesty and truth from others around them, especially their leaders.

- To be valued for their quality work and their precise opinions.

- Details, details, and then some more details.

- Things to make sense.

Connection Points:

1. In the South we say, "Have your ducks in a row!" This means you have thought through the process and have

the details in place in a way that makes sense. The language of a C style is detailed information. If you're not a detailed person, you need to spend some intentional time getting that way with whatever it is you're wanting to speak to the C type about. It is better to wait and have more details than it is to engage without enough specifics in place. Also, understand that regardless of how much detail you bring to the table, the C style will probably want more or will research some more themselves to provide them.

2. Don't ever tell them "You're wrong." That's absolutely the *worst* phrase you can say to a C. Remember that they'd rather be anything but wrong and have worked extremely hard not to be incorrect. If you ever throw this phrase out, you'd better be ready for World War III in the form of information. They're going to pull out forms and documents that would rival the IRS code and go page by page, telling you why they're right.

   Conversely, if they are truly wrong, and you can prove it, they will eventually admit their mistake. They won't like it. It's severe pain for them, but they will admit it, given enough evidence. If you're in that situation, be as gracious as possible, knowing you're encountering one of the most painful situations they'll ever experience.

3. Be truthful, even if you think it will hurt. Remember that they usually aren't emotional people, so telling them the truth isn't hurting their feelings. Lying to them, even to save their feelings, will break their trust, and trust for C types is difficult to build and even more difficult to rebuild. Be totally honest, and keep in mind—most of the time—a C, like many parents with a child, is already aware of the truth and is just waiting for you to tell them.

4. Don't engage in small talk. Get to the purpose of why you're there. Small talk is a waste of time for them. As we said previously, they have their time preplanned and view it as highly valuable.

5. View interactions as a business meeting. Avoid personal questions. C types are normally closed to talking about personal information and issues unless they know someone very well. Even then, they normally will not engage in personal conversations when there is work to be done.

6. C types crave information and details. You cannot give them enough. You cannot overload them. The more details you give them, the more they'll appreciate your preparation and *you.*

7. Make sure you have quality answers prepared. Quality answers are well thought out and detailed in nature. It is infinitely better to tell a C type, "I'm not sure, and I don't want to tell you the wrong thing" than it is to tell them something that may or may not be accurate. When in doubt, go research it, then come back and talk to them. They'll respect you more if you do.

8. Don't interrupt them when they're talking to you. Not only is it disrespectful, it also screams at them that you don't value their opinion. If you do, they'll likely stop talking altogether.

9. Trust is earned in pennies and spent in dollars. While this is true of all styles, you especially don't want to violate this maxim with a C type. If you have violated their trust, apologize first. They're waiting for you to come around and admit your mistake. And do it sooner rather than later.

10. You will probably get one of two responses from a C style: One, silence. This means they're listening and analyzing. Don't take it as a negative. Take it as normal. Two, they will ask "Why?" Again—realize this isn't pushback. It's actually a good thing for you in that they want to know more about what you're proposing.

11. Don't expect instant answers from a C. Remember, they are **cautious** people who don't make snap decisions.

Expect them to say something like, "I need some time to think about this." They research and research some more. Tell them what you need and then say, "I want to give you the time I know you need to research this. If I haven't given you enough information, feel free to follow up with me for more." And then, expect them to follow up and then DO give them more. Be prepared for all of your meetings with a C personality!

Phrases a C personality loves to hear:

"I really value your opinion."

"That was PERFECT!"

"I love how you think."

"Thank you for handling that with such detail and precision."

"I trust you."

"What do you think about this?"

"Can you research this for me?"

And a big one when communicating with a C style: "You have an incredible grasp of this subject. Please give me more details about this so I can understand it better and learn from you."

How do you deal with a C type out of control? Some older people may remember the recording when you called an incorrect number.

"The number you dialed is not a working number. If you feel you've reached this recording in error, please check the number and dial again."

The message is basically saying, "You called the wrong number. If you think you're right, you're not. Now hang up and do it right the next time." This message was written by a C personality.

This is what you're facing when confronting an out-of-control C. They are utterly convinced they are right. When they are pushed out of control, they detach emotionally and move into a robotic state. You must approach them with cold, hard facts. Emotions will accomplish nothing and will only drive them further away. They must be convinced with details, facts, and logic. Emphasize your desire for things to run with excellence and that you, like them, want this to be as perfect as possible. As a reserved person, they will not respond well to an over-the-top, outgoing approach either. Keep everything factual and emphasize (with details to back them up!) the desire to accomplish the task with excellence.

Style Tips for Connecting with a C:

If you're a D:

- You both connect on the task side of things. You're both not fans of "touchy-feely" stuff. Tell them specifically the task you want to accomplish and, more importantly, WHY you want to accomplish it.

- You're used to bottom-line points. But keep in mind, bullet points don't work well with C styles. They need explanations and details for what you're giving.

- When they ask "Why?"—and they will—don't take that as a challenge to your authority. It isn't. A C will ask "Why" because it is their nature, and they *must* know!

- Because of their desire for detail, budget more time for this meeting and remember that you and your team will be more productive and have a better result because of the contribution of this person. Their input makes you and your team win!

- Let them know you value their opinion as well as their attention to accuracy and details.

- Don't take it personally if they disagree with you. That's their nature—to question. Don't engage in a debate. If you don't have a ton of details prepared, you're not ready to debate them anyway. It's better to find common ground on what you *do* agree on than it is to waste time on what you don't.

If you're an I:

- Realize that you and the C are polar opposites. This means as an I, out of all the temperaments, you and the C types have the least in common.

- Realize that what you find funny and fun, they can find to be a waste of valuable time. A C greatly values their time, and they don't like it to be wasted with frivolity or silliness.

- Get to the point of why you're there with them.

- Don't focus on your feelings and don't ask them for theirs. Remember—they're logical people who process through their minds (thus the title of this chapter!). The way to connect with them is through logic and through your mind.

- I types are not naturally detail focused. To speak to a C, you <u>must</u> be. Spend extra time (days, even weeks) to prepare for this meeting. If you go in halfway prepared, expect a short meeting with little productivity and a good long while before they'll have another meeting with you.

- Don't take it personally if they aren't smiling.

- Don't take it personally if they are not responding but are listening to you in silence instead. It doesn't mean they don't like you. In fact, it's actually a good thing. They're processing what you're saying and waiting politely for you to finish.

- Don't take it personally if they disagree with you. That's their nature—to question. Don't engage in a debate. If you don't have a ton of details prepared, you're not ready to debate them anyway. It's better to find common ground on what you *do* agree on than it is to waste time on what you don't.

- When you think you've acquired enough details to talk to a C, stop. Double your details, then go talk to them. Also, realize that the huge amount of details you gave them still wasn't enough. Don't take it personally! That's just their style.

- You'll have bonus points with a C if you have all your details typed out with a copy for them to keep.

- Resist every urge you have to interrupt them when they're talking—even if you disagree. That's rude. You must let them finish their thoughts completely. C types do not waste words. They mean what they say and say what they mean. If you interrupt them, you're screaming to them that you don't truly care about what they're saying. They will stop talking and will not see the point of trying to talk again.

- Don't communicate with a C to receive affirmation. Affirmation from a C is a job well done with excellence and is generally not verbalized. If you do get a compliment from a C style, don't take it for granted. It's like a precious diamond—exceedingly rare.

If you're an S:

- You and the C are both reserved, which can make some communication parts challenging if neither of you talk.

- Realize that you're helping them by being more assertive in what you want.

- Realize that you're serving them by having a ton of details related to why you're there.

- Listen to what they say. Tell them you want to learn from them and then truly listen to them. You're already a great listener. Use that gift to connect with them.

- Once you get the details, make sure you understand it. If you didn't understand it, ask them to repeat it so you can be sure. Not only are they willing to repeat it for clarity's sake, they'll also appreciate your desire to get it right and be excellent in your work.

- Work diligently and give progress reports. Expect further details and instructions and maybe even a few course corrections. You're a great finisher and are a highly valuable member of this team. It will mean a great deal to the C styles that you finish the work they give you, according to their specific details, with excellence. Whether they verbalize it or not, they'll be extremely glad you're on their team.

If you're a C:

- You both value hard work, excellence, quality answers, and details.

- You both want to do things the right way.

- The potential conflict here is when you disagree about exactly what the "right way" is. Consider that your way may not be the only way. (Don't swing at us for suggesting that!)

- Be willing to listen and entertain the idea that there could be more than one right way to accomplish something and still do it with excellence!

During my years in ministry, there was one person in particular who I had a hard time working with—not because they were a bad person. They weren't. In fact, they were remarkably good. And the disagreement didn't come from the normal place of being task-oriented versus people-oriented. In truth, we are both task-oriented personalities. The conflict wasn't even about the methodology. We knew we had a job to do and agreed that it had to be completed by a certain time.

So why the conflict?

It was because this person's tendency was to step in and do the work for everybody (including me). As I said at the beginning of the book, I call that "Finger-in-my-Fruit-Loops Syndrome," and I don't like it. I don't want or need somebody doing my work for me. And as a predominantly D personality style, I took it as them questioning my abilities and competency.

But that's not at all what they were doing.

Our methods were the same, but our *intents* were different. Even though we are both task-oriented, I was working for results and to win. They were working to do the project in the right way and the way that, in their mind, was done with excellence. That's where we parted ways.

In their mind, I was moving so fast that the work wasn't excellent, and there were some obvious mistakes. In my mind, they were taking so much time poring over pedantic details that they were slowing everything and everybody else down and even redoing some of my work that (again—in my mind) did not need to be redone.

So—who was right?

We **both** were *right*. And we **both** were *wrong*.

Once I understood the different temperaments, I understood this person wasn't working against me. They were simply trying to keep me from making costly errors that, in the end, would require me to have to redo things and take even more time. I should have relied more on their attention to details and expertise.

They should have respected the work I had done more and talked to me before merely stepping in and undoing everything. The initial work I did could have been built upon. Also, if they had talked to me, I could have learned and grown some more.

And the scenario I just described—the one that should have happened—actually <u>did</u> happen. And we became the best of friends. We went from looking at each other with suspicion and resentment to demonstrating mutual respect for our gifts, and an understanding of our intents and mutual desire to accomplish something significant.

C styles are the brains of the organizations. We need them to do things in the most efficient, compliant, and effective way. We can learn from them. We can appreciate them.

The Bible tells us that renewing our minds is a major key to being who Christ wants us to be:

"And do not be conformed to this world, but be transformed by the renewing of your mind, that you may prove what is that good and acceptable and perfect will of God" (Romans 12:2 NKJV).

All of us can use some renewing in our minds. And many of our C friends know how to lead us there. We need them in our lives!

11

CONNECTING WITH THE STRENGTH

Donna (not her real name) was a high-powered head of one of the largest and highest producing businesses in the South. They did billions in business every year. So when I was recommended to her as a speaker for her next event, I was told to wait in a hallway for her to come by. I waited patiently and saw her turn the corner. She was flanked on both sides by a man and a woman, who were obviously near her to serve her needs.

As she got close to me, the man spoke to her and said, "Donna, this is Ken, the speaker they were telling you about."

Donna took one look at me and then blurted out, "You have thirty seconds to tell me why I should let you speak to my people at our next event."

I knew the language of who I was talking to, and I knew exactly what to say. The clues were all there in that three-second sentence. She spoke an imperative order to me with a time limit: "You have thirty seconds." "Tell me why I should let you speak to MY people."

Donna was large and in charge.

I didn't even pause. I looked her in the eyes (even though she wasn't looking me in the eyes at the time) and replied, "If I could help all of your people understand themselves and their coworkers in a way that they never have before, where they get along better and it causes your productivity to go through the roof in the next twelve months, would that be of value to you?"

Donna's eyes cut to mine, and we made eye contact. She asked, "Exactly how are you going to do that?"

I replied with a grin, "To tell you that, I need two minutes of your time."

She smiled back at me and said, "I'll give you three."

Even though she said three minutes, I stuck to my quote of two minutes and actually only took ninety seconds to briefly explain my keynote address, using bullet points and emphasizing the results of each one. I booked that meeting on the spot. It was one of my first big speaking gigs that paid extremely well, and I booked it because I spoke the language of strength.

D types bring strength to the table and move organizations forward in shorter amounts of time than other temperaments can do in years. They can appear invincible, but they definitely have pain points like every other temperament.

Pain Points:

1. A life with no challenge. A D personality needs a challenge, like all of us need air to breathe. Without it, they suffocate.

2. Being bossed around. If you want to rub a D personality the wrong way, simply boss them around. Resentment will start to build; and, if it's left unchecked, it could turn to anger or even rage.

3. Telling them they "can't do something." I don't just mean rules and regulations. I mean, if they lay out a goal and you tell them "That's just not possible"—GAME ON. Now they're going to do it just to prove you wrong.

4. Not giving them the opportunity for choices and control over something. This is another suffocating point. Maybe their experience only qualifies them to oversee something minor for a period of time. Fine. But giving them something to be in charge of is better than nothing at all.

5. Lack of direction. This drives a D type up a wall. For example, think about four people in a car, only one of

whom is a D type. The others are discussing where they want to eat and cannot decide where it should be. They discuss and discuss and then change their mind; and then, they discuss some more, get off topic, and then come back and talk some more… You get the idea. This is a short road for a blowup for a D type, who will probably stand up and yell, "Just get in the car and let me drive!" The lack of decision and direction will become unbearable for them very quickly.

Misperception Points:

Please keep in mind as you read these that we are *not* saying this is how anyone actually is. We're simply saying this is how others could misperceive you. But let's be real here; do you really care that much about what they think about you anyway? Yep. Thought not.

1. D types can be seen as dictators. They're barking orders at people without considering anyone's feelings. In their quest to get results right now, they often forget the personality styles involved and the essential contributions they're making to the organization.

2. D types can be seen as insensitive and rude. This comes from their penchant for being extremely direct, especially when asked for an opinion about something. In their minds, they're simply being honest. In many others' minds, their behavior is rude.

3. Arrogant. D types have a natural self-confidence. They know what they're good at, and they stick to it. They also have strong opinions and stick to those as well . . . to the death. Having confidence in one's abilities to perform is not the same thing as arrogance. The real test is why they're doing it and how they're using their abilities. Is it solely for them? That's arrogance. Is it to benefit others or the organization? That's usually confidence.

4. Jerks. Combine all three of the above misperceptions and you have all the makings of what people would

consider to be a jerk. It's never the intention, but in the drive to succeed, make things happen, and get results, D types can occasionally miss the bodies they're leaving behind on the side of the road. They need to shift their focus to people to make sure they're not leaving everyone behind.

"A leader who has no followers isn't leading. They're merely taking a walk." – Dr. John C. Maxwell

Desires:

A D style is looking for:

- Respect. This is a primary need. If this need isn't met, don't expect a D to hang around long in your organization.

- Challenges. D types thrive on challenges and need them. If they're not continually challenged with new and exciting tasks, they'll become bored and seek out a different and more challenging position.

- Variety. D types also enjoy a variety of tasks and challenges. You're not going to overwhelm them. What others would shy away from, they'll face head-on, and not only get past it, but they'll also conquer it. I mean *obliterate* it.

- The truth. Don't beat around the bush. Don't imply it and then say, "Well, surely they read between the lines!" D types don't read between the lines. They read exactly what's on the page. They expect communication with them to be the same manner that they communicate. Blunt, to the point, and brutally honest.

- Results. They want to win. Don't believe me? Bobby Knight was the basketball coach for the Indiana Hoosiers and an off-the-scale D type. His claim to fame is becoming so passionate about the game they were losing that he threw a chair in the middle of the basketball court and was tossed from the game. Wrong actions? Yes. Passionate to win? OH yeah! Some of the best coaches in any sport today are D types because sports is ultimately about winning, and D styles know how to get that done.

- Control. If nobody is "driving," expect the D to volunteer (so to speak). They'd rather get moving down the road and will gladly take the reins if nobody else is. But more than that, they do need to have a measure of control in some areas of their life. To deny them, this will deny who they are meant to be.

- Clear goals and measurable results.

- Actions. They don't respect words without actions to back them up. They don't just talk about ideas and dreams. They *achieve* them.

Connection Points:

1. Be firm. Don't be wishy-washy in your delivery. It should be firm and with confidence. If you don't believe in what you're saying, then why should they?

2. Be direct. Whether it feels rude to you or not, say it directly and bluntly. Don't imply anything. Just flat out say it if you want them to get it.

3. Be brief. Don't beat around the bush. Get to the point. Quickly.

4. Ask for their opinion on something if you're not sure about it. I promise you, they have an opinion, and if they don't have one at that moment, they can shortly come up with one if asked.

5. Remember that D styles are goal and results oriented. If they don't know the reason you're there and what you're trying to accomplish, they'll likely turn you off and move on to another task as quickly as possible.

6. If you don't get to the point of what you want within the first fifteen to twenty seconds of your conversation, they'll also likely check out. Again—get to the point quickly and bluntly.

7. Find ways to convey how what you're doing or wanting will be a win for them and for the team. How does it move the team closer to their goals?

8. If you're supervising a D type and giving them instructions, give bottom-line, bullet-point instructions instead of extraneous details. They'll fill in the blanks they need or will ask for further clarifications.

9. Like a thoroughbred horse, allow the D types to run. Let them come up with action plans. Let them move things forward. If something is "stuck" in your organization, let the D step in, and it won't remain stuck for long. If you give them this freedom, you'll connect with them, and they will not forget the opportunity you gave them to shine and succeed.

How do you deal with an out-of-control D? Sound the alarm! Hide under the furniture! An out-of-control D comes out swinging and raging. Although they are task-side people, this emotion of rage can take charge and result in them saying very mean things. At this point, it's best for you to get out of the way and leave them alone. Given time by themselves, the anger will subside. Remember that they are logical people, and you will have a chance to appeal to that logic, but not while they're raging. Give them time to calm down. How much? They'll wear this rage on their face and their demeanor. You'll know. Once they calm down, reinforce your desire to help them win and make it clear you're on their side. Tell them you respect their passion and power. They desire respect and results. Let them know you're on the team with them to help them achieve their goals.

Phrases a D personality loves to hear:

"Way to go!"

"I really respect you!"

"Well done!"

"Thanks for your strong leadership!"

"You win!"

"It's your choice. You're in charge."

"Can you give me some direction here?"

"What do you think?"

"I would really respect your opinion."

And the ultimate: "You totally conquered that goal! It didn't stand a chance against you!"

Style Tips for Connecting with a D:

If you're a D:

- This is going to be a powerhouse encounter with lots of hand gestures and lots of volume!

- It's also likely going to be a short meeting, because you both have other important things you need to get done.

- The potential problem comes from one of two things: One, you disagree with how something should be done; or two, you feel like one is challenging the authority of the other. In either case, sound the alarm and get ready for a nuclear blast! Okay, maybe not that drastic, but it can be a volatile situation.

- Consider that every idea has some validity and hearing someone out, whether you use their idea or not, is a way of showing something that you, yourself desire: respect.

- Realize that meeting in the middle and compromising help you get results and achieve the win. In other words, the goal is to win the war, not every single battle. Choose wisely. Winning a small debate will not be worth it if you end up losing your ultimate goal because of it.

- Situations of authority require different responses. If you're in authority over the other person, don't use a title or intimidation. Those are the weakest points from which you can lead. Your goal is to win and get results, and you need a team to do it. Spread the credit to your team.

- If someone else oversees you, it is important for you to stay under that authority and show respect to the person, even if you disagree. Someday, it may be you in charge, and you will want that same respect.

If you're an I:

- You're both outgoing, which means you both like to talk. This can be good or bad. As an I, you like to talk about different things. Realize that a D is only interested in talking about things that will help them achieve their goal of getting results. In other words, always engage a D in purposeful conversations, not small talk.

- Avoid interrupting a D. They'll take it as a sign of disrespect, and that's always a bad thing to convey to a D. This applies to conversations as well as unannounced drop-in meetings and phone calls. It's always best to make an appointment if you need to talk to a D. It shows respect for their time.

- Avoid going in with needless humor. They will consider it a waste of time, and a D's time is of utmost importance to them. Don't waste it with dialogue that doesn't have a specific purpose for *them*.

- Don't talk to the D in stories or extraneous anecdotes. Talk to them in short bullet points. Get there quickly. If you've taken longer than three minutes to convey your point, you've likely already lost them. If they want more information or need it, they'll ask you for it.

- Don't say it in ten words when you could have said it in five. Be concise.

- Don't take it personally if they're not smiling or not in a joking mood. It doesn't mean they don't like you; it may simply mean they're focused on the task at hand (D types can have a laser focus) and don't want to "waste time" on things that don't move them toward their goal.

- Never ask them how they "feel" about something. They don't feel. They think. They process through the filter of logic, not emotions.

- Have your agenda prepared before you walk into that meeting with a D.

- Never ask for a meeting with a D without telling them "what" the meeting is about. "I want to meet with you about _____" is the proper way to ask for a meeting. If you don't tell them what the meeting is for, expect to be met with suspicion or even a decline.

If you're an S:

- Realize that you and the D are polar opposites. This means as an S, out of all the temperaments, you and the D types have the least in common.

- Whatever reason you're there for, get to the main point quickly. Avoid extraneous details or personal conversation. It may seem rude to you not to ask, "How are you doing?" but to a D type, asking that question is intrusive and could be perceived as small talk and a waste of time.

- Clear your throat and speak up. This is going to go against everything in your nature, but it is necessary to do when talking to them.

- Realize that what you consider rude, they consider being straight-forward and blunt. Don't be afraid to speak your mind. They'll appreciate your candor.

- Maintain eye contact. Looking down or looking away could be taken as a sign of weakness or even dishonesty.

- It is your nature to be humble, but in this case, confidence will speak louder to a D type. Avoid saying "I'll try" and replace that with "I will," but—you *must* follow through with what you say you'll do to maintain their respect. Remember, they respect action and results more than words and promises.

- Be brief and be firm.

- Don't say it in ten words when you could have said it in five. Be concise.

- D types enjoy dreams and challenges. Talk about new strategies and ideas with them. They'll likely embrace them.

- Talk with conviction.

- When the conversation is done (which is normally pretty quickly), look them in the eyes, thank them for their time, and walk out. Again—all this may seem rude to you, but you must remember that you're communicating in the way *they* prefer to be communicated with, not the way *you* prefer.

- Avoid unannounced drop-in meetings or phone calls. A D type will think it's disrespectful, and because you interrupted them, you won't get the attention and quality time you're desiring. Make an appointment to speak with them. It'll not only show them you respect them, but you'll also get more quality answers.

If you're a C:

- You both connect on the task side of things, so this conversation will connect in that realm.

- Don't say it in ten words when you could have said it in five. Be concise. Even if it means sacrificing details you feel you must tell them, get to the bottom line quickly. It shouldn't feel like you're a lawyer making a case for a plaintiff. Instead, think of this as a thirty-second commercial.

- To reiterate, the details you feel are essential may be optional for them. This one point will be where you'll struggle the most in communicating with them.

- Instead of focusing on the process, focus on the outcome and goals. D types pay much more attention to the results and don't care as much about the process. After all, that's what *you're* there for!

- Prioritize your details into these four categories: A) Must know—it won't work without this. B) Need to know—these are priorities they should know. C) Would be nice to know—these will make things more efficient, and D) Things that would make it "perfect." Now realize—you will likely only get to point "A" with a D type, and that's Okay. Make sure those "A" details are the critical ones.

For example, you see someone is in a wreck; and you're a doctor, and you see they have a broken arm; their shoulder is bleeding, and they have gone into cardiac arrest. The first two issues aren't as critical. The heart attack must be addressed first. As a C type, speaking to a D type, prioritize the critical details first with the understanding that you may never get to the other ones. Likely, they'll leave the other details to you or someone else to handle.

- If you press for an answer, you'll likely get one, but it may not be the quality one you need. Encourage them to take a little time to consider their answer. Let them know your desire is to use a well-thought-out response so you can ensure you have what you need to help them get the best result they are looking for. Snap decisions are often not the highest quality ones, simply because they're trying to check something off their list.

- D types have a natural problem-solving ability. You may not agree with the process, but that's Okay. They may not agree with the process either and may be extremely open to your input on it. They simply want the problem solved to keep moving forward.

- A D type of person thrives on respect. Showing respect, even in the face of disagreement, will earn you the right to be heard.

- Your logical explanations will be a big connection point with a D. Lay out a logical action plan, emphasizing goals and results.

- Any type of confrontation should be done face-to-face. Emails or voice mails can come across as cowardly. When you confront a D type, lead with caring and respect for their authority and temperament.

- If you think they're wrong, don't blurt out, "That's wrong." It'll be taken as a challenge to their authority, and a D is always up for a fight. (I don't mean physically . . . but with a D . . . you never know.) The best approach is to be polite and say, "I disagree," for whatever reason. They appreciate direct, but respectful responses. You also need to accept that they may disagree with you. If the conversation degrades into a debate, your goal of doing things correctly will become lost in the shuffle of them trying to "win."

D types can have issues connecting with others. Many times, they're an island, and they prefer it that way; but sometimes they're an island and don't know how they got that way. They may have stories of how other people are mad at them "for no reason," and they "don't understand why or what they ever did to them." And what they're saying is true. They don't know the reason. They don't understand it. They were just being themselves, doing their thing, and inadvertently offended someone who wrote them off and quit talking to them. The tragedy is, they may never know why and may lose a connection permanently because of their lack of awareness.

I heard William Shatner interviewed recently, and he threw out several of these statements about former cast members he worked with throughout his career. While the cast members may have not formally addressed their grievances with Mr. Shatner, they most definitely addressed them in other public interviews. He was described as **demanding**, **dictatorial,** ordering others around (like a **director**), and **dogmatic** in his stances on how things should be done on the sets. Can you say, "D type"? And yet, his accomplishments throughout his career speak for themselves. Denny Crane, T.J. Hooker, and (of course) Captain James T. Kirk are all iconic character creations that will never be duplicated. A D type out of control can produce results; but at the same time, they can also be bad at connecting with others.

And yet, despite the occasional carnage they leave in their wake, we need them. We need their direction. We need their action. We need their strength, especially during hard times. Give them a crisis, and not only will they push through it, but they'll also blaze a pathway for others to follow.

The Body of Christ needs those D types in order to bring strength to the table for the greater good of everyone. D types need to learn that the true source of their strength isn't in their independence, but rather in their dependence on the Lord. The more they rely on Him, the stronger they are for everyone else. And if we're truly loving our D "neighbors" as we love ourselves, we'll help them do it.

> *"Finally, my brethren, be strong in the Lord and in the power of His might"* (Ephesians 6:10, NKJV).

12

HOW JESUS COMMUNICATED AND CONNECTED

In the first chapter, we demonstrated several examples of how Jesus communicated in various styles when it fit different situations and needs. We often refer to the DISC styles as "languages," because our styles simply impact how we naturally communicate.

Ultimately, your goal should be to learn how to speak each of the four languages of DISC. When you can do that, you have established the foundation needed to become a master communicator. As Ken mentioned earlier, it is highly unlikely that the average person will speak all the languages fluently. But even if you speak another style's language with a "thick accent," they will most likely appreciate the effort made.

When we speak to someone in a language they understand, we connect to their mind. When we speak to them in their native language, we connect with their heart.

I remember speaking to a large outdoor crowd in the Dominican Republic. I had an interpreter assigned to me who was going to help translate the message for me as I spoke. While I speak some Spanish, I would hardly call myself "fluent" in the language. During the afternoon, I sat down and wrote out my opening comments and had my interpreter help translate everything for me so it would be understood in their dialect. Then I memorized my opening in Spanish for that evening. I remember telling him, "You'd better be close. After this statement, I need you." We both got a laugh out of that.

After I spoke that evening, he remarked about how that was received by the crowd. He told me he had never seen someone do that before. Oh, trust me, they knew it was definitely not my primary language, but the fact that I spoke to them in their language at the very beginning really helped me connect with them. That is really all we are doing with DISC.

Don't miss this point. Everyone speaks a language that is driven by their personality style, whether they have ever been "trained" in it or not. It just happens naturally. And I can promise you, just because you both "speak English" does NOT mean you speak the same language. Hey men (because I am wise enough not to say this to the ladies!), how many of you have ever had your spouse or significant other say something like, "That is not anything close to what I said at all!"? Yep, I thought so. See, even though you might have both been speaking English, you weren't really speaking the same language.

One of the biggest mistakes I see leaders make is when they try to speak to everyone the same way. I usually hear some form of the statement, "I'm the leader. They should adapt to me." There is so much wrong with that statement that I won't even attempt to fix it here, but that is a sign of a leader who is headed for serious trouble.

Jesus adjusted His style of communication to fit the situation and/or person needed at the moment.

> **Heart-** In Matthew 19 is the account where the children were all being brought to Jesus. I can just picture them climbing on Him and having fun as He laid His hands on them. The disciples tried to rebuke them and make them stop, but Jesus stopped them in their tracks. Just imagine if He had pushed them away because He "didn't have time for all that." I wonder if it would have impacted how He was received. I believe that if He had done that, people would have seen Him as arrogant and aloof. They already knew what that was like. The crowds were drawn to Him like a magnet, partly because everything about Him was different from what they experienced from all the so-called religious leaders of the day.

> **Soul-** When Jesus was being crucified on the cross, there were two thieves hanging next to Him as well. One of them

scoffed at Him, but the other did not. He asked Jesus to remember him. Jesus told him that he would be with Him in paradise that day. How do you think it would have been received if Jesus had started listing all the man's sins to him? It wasn't like there was anything the man could do about it at that point. Then again, that man represents every one of us. There is nothing we could do to absolve our sins either, except to rely on His sacrifice and mercy to reconcile us to God. Some things never change.

Mind- In chapter 5 of Luke, we read about the account where a group of men lowered a paralyzed man through the roof down to Jesus. Seeing their faith, Jesus told him, *"Man, your sins are forgiven"* (Luke 5:20, NKJV).

Like a broken record, the religious leaders were upset. How dare He think He could forgive someone's sins? Only God alone could do that. Hmm. I think they were missing the point there. But okay, Jesus gave them a rational statement about whether it was easier to say one thing or the other. He was addressing their "list of rules" head-on and showing that a relationship would always outweigh them. To be clear, that is not a negative statement about rules. C types love rules. But these leaders valued their list of man-made rules above what the Son of God was doing right in their very midst. Yes, rules matter, but we have to be able to see the big picture as well and not allow a list of rules to cause us to miss a move of God.

If Jesus had not been able to match their "logic" point for point, I wonder if the faith of the men who brought the man to Jesus would have failed. And that faith is why he was healed that day.

Strength- Before he was called Paul, the apostle was once known as Saul. While traveling on the road to Damascus in Acts 9, Saul had an encounter with Jesus that would change his life. Additionally, this defining moment also had a tremendous impact on the growth of the church as a whole. Saul was literally traveling to Damascus to persecute the believers, but he had an experience like nothing else.

"As he journeyed he came near Damascus, and suddenly a light shone around him from heaven. Then he fell to the ground, and heard a voice saying to him, 'Saul, Saul, why are you persecuting me?' And he said, 'Who are You, Lord?' Then the Lord said, 'I am Jesus, whom you are persecuting. It is hard for you to kick against the goads.' So he, trembling and astonished, said, 'Lord what do You want me to do?' Then the Lord said to him, 'Arise and go into the city, and you will be told what you must do'" (Acts 9:3–6, NKJV).

Saul had a very direct personality style. Jesus knew that, and therefore, that was exactly how He communicated with him. He basically had to knock him off his horse to get his attention. Just imagine if He had tried to speak gently and softly to Saul. Saul would have taken that as a sign of weakness, and their interaction would likely have ended with a very different outcome.

As a high D myself, I know He has spoken to me many times just like that. As you have probably (and hopefully) seen numerous times throughout this book, it just goes to show that we have all been God-Wired in unique ways, yet in ways that can help us learn how to communicate effectively with others to truly connect with them based on their individual styles.

My Favorite Example

The Gospel of John provides one of the most powerful examples I've seen in the Bible about how we need to communicate to people differently based on their personality styles.

In John chapter 11, we read about the account of the death and ultimate resurrection of Lazarus. I encourage you to read the entire story, but there is a point here that is truly fascinating.

Jesus arrived in Bethany, where Lazarus had died. Both of Lazarus's sisters, Martha and Mary, were there. Martha heard that He was coming first. She went out to meet Him. Perk your antennas up. You don't want to miss this.

"Now Martha said to Jesus, 'Lord, if You had been here, my brother would not have died'" (John 11:21, NKJV).

Anytime Martha is mentioned, we can clearly see she is definitely a task-oriented person. Jesus responded to her with the truth of the Gospel. They basically had a theological discussion. Martha was a "logic-first" type of person. Her mind was broken, so Jesus spoke directly to her in an intellectual fashion.

Now, skim down the chapter eleven verses and take a look at verse 32. By this time, Martha had gone and told Mary that Jesus was calling for her. So she went to Him. Look at what happened next.

"Then, when Mary came where Jesus was, and saw Him, she fell down at His feet, saying to Him, 'Lord, if You had been here, my brother would not have died'" (John 11:32, NKJV).

Wait a minute. Did I just write the wrong thing by mistake? That sentence looks just like the one I wrote above. I mean, exactly. As in, word for word!

But the following reaction from Jesus was *very* different. Following this interaction, "Jesus wept."

As we can see, any time Mary is mentioned, she is a very emotion-first type of person. Jesus responded to her with compassion and emotion. She didn't need "truth" at that moment. She needed to know that He felt the hurt and pain like she did. Mary was an "emotion-first" type of person. Her heart was broken, so He connected with her at an emotional level.

This is a lesson in what it looks like to become a Master Communicator. Jesus knew how we have been God-Wired. The signs are often there for us all. The main thing is that we need to be willing to adapt accordingly.

How We Connect with God

We connect with God in different ways as well. To be crystal clear here, I am NOT talking about how we get to Heaven. There is only one way to God, and that is through Jesus Christ.

"I am the way, the truth, and the life. No one comes to the Father, except through Me" (John 14:6, NKJV).

Just so we are clear, those are His words, not ours. Jesus did not leave that statement any room for doubt or other interpretation.

That said, we do connect with Him differently. Some people connect with Him on an emotional level. They love the emotion of worship, for example. They love the fellowship. They cry during worship, a testimony, a prayer, and/or a message. They love those "moments" where you can tangibly feel God's presence.

Others connect with God on a logical level. They live for a deep dive into the truths of the word of God. They want to go as deep as the deepest part of the ocean into a book of the Bible, and swim there for a while as they gather every single mind-blowing truth. They leave those moments feeling they have a renewed mind.

I believe it is important to note that one of these external expressions is not any more or less authentic than the other. It is not that one type feels emotion and the other doesn't; but rather, it is that they express the emotion they are feeling differently in an outward manner. Perhaps that is why it is so important that God looks at our hearts!

We also see this in churches. There are churches that are predominantly emotionally based, and others that are predominantly logically based. It's likely because "birds of a feather flock together," and we naturally gravitate to people who seem similar to us. But are we losing something in our churches today by doing this? Paul, in I Corinthians 12, encourages diversity and unity in the Body of Christ. And unity doesn't mean everyone thinks and connects the same way. It's actually the opposite. It's the ability to be different and yet come together through our mutual connection to God through a relationship with Jesus Christ. Whether we connect more logically or emotionally shouldn't keep us from bonding!

So if your question is, "Well, which one is valid?" The answer is, they *both* are. And one should not despise the other.

If you read the Psalms, it is abundantly clear that David connected with God on a deeply emotional level. His Psalms are packed with a range of emotions, from passionate love to deep-seated anger. God called David a man after His own heart.

If you read the epistles of Paul, he clearly connects with God on a deeply logical level. Walking with God is the most logical thing he could have done. Once he understood everything Jesus had done for him, what choice did he have but to follow Him? And Paul's writings to the churches and Timothy show his fierce, systematic, theological defense of Jesus the Christ.

Both men were greatly used by God. Both were men of God. They simply connected with Him in different ways.

The lesson is clear. Don't despise how you are God-Wired! If you connect with God emotionally, enjoy the emotional, impassioned journey to God's heart. If you enjoy clearing out the clutter of this world and diving deep into the Bible to draw out deep spiritual lessons and truths, that's great too. Lead on and discover those truths that help others understand God in a deeper way.

The point is, whether it's more emotional or logical, we should strive to connect with God in a way that is true and real for us.

Don't try to change your personality style. Regardless of what blend you have or where you plot on a personality graph, know that you have been God-Wired just the way He wanted you. Just learn to adapt the way you communicate to others so you can effectively communicate with them and foster strong relationships, but you have been uniquely and wonderfully made, just the way you are. You have a GREAT personality! God bless!

CHAPTER 13

CONCLUSION

All of us have a primary style, but we are all blends of all four temperaments in varying degrees. You can develop in your weakest areas, but you'll always be weaker in that area because it doesn't come naturally, like your strengths do.

Here are a few parting tips for your primary styles:

If your primary style is an I, remember:

- Being more businesslike will help others to take you more seriously.

- Resist the urge to be led by just your feelings when completing projects. Other styles will need something more concrete than simply your feelings.

- Take the time to listen and pay attention without interrupting.

- The biggest skill you can develop is *accuracy*. Be accurate in your answers and avoid exaggerating. It will prove to people (especially task-oriented people) that you are truthful and trustworthy.

- Do what you say. Your actions will speak louder than your words every time.

- There is a time for play and a time for work. Sometimes, those lines blur, but it doesn't happen very often when you're dealing with task-oriented people.

- Keep in mind that seventy percent of the population does not process things the way you do. Be willing to adjust to them and speak their language to connect.

- Being more task-oriented at times will not only help you accomplish more, but you'll enjoy your successes and have more time for fun and connections.

If your primary style is an S, remember:

- Set boundaries for yourself so people don't walk all over you and take advantage of you. There is a difference between a servant and a doormat.

- Resist the urge to agree with everything everybody says.

- Let others take responsibility for their own actions. You can't fix or save everybody.

- The biggest skill you can develop is being more *assertive*.

- Being honest and open actually helps others.

- Don't be afraid to express your true opinions. Your opinion needs to be heard.

- Keep in mind that sixty-five percent of the population does not process things the way you do. Be willing to adjust to them and speak their language to connect.

- Being more task-oriented at times can help your team, serve their needs, finish more projects, and create more peace at your workplace.

If your primary style is a C, remember:

- Resist the tendency to give too many details. While you thrive on details, it confuses others. In listening to *all* the details, the details that are the *most* important can be lost.

- Look at the overall goal, narrow down the absolute bare bones of what is necessary to achieve that goal, and then communicate that.

- Use your keen intellect and intelligence to encourage other people.

- Smile. It won't kill you. It *will* help you connect.

- The biggest skill you can develop is being more *flexible*.

- Rather than communicating the entire process, try focusing on the end results and clearly explaining how they should look. Doing so may cause your team members to buy into your plan more than a list of details and processes.

- Adapt your communication and expectation to the primary style of each team member. It will be different for each one.

- Consider that the feelings of other people may very well be different from yours.

- Keep in mind that seventy-five percent of the population doesn't process things the way you do. If you want to connect, you'll have to adjust to them and speak their languages.

- Being more people-oriented at times and thinking about how others feel will help you be more efficient, more effective, and make your work even more excellent.

If your primary style is a D, remember:

- Allow others to take the lead and have authority.

- Before you can be in authority, you must learn to be under authority.

- The biggest skill you can develop is the ability to *yield* when necessary.

- Smile. It won't kill you. It *will* help you connect.

- Take time to relax and recharge. There is nothing noble or spiritual about working all the time.

- Prioritize your personal life over your work. You must have balance.

- Keep in mind that ninety percent of the population doesn't process things the way you do. If you want to connect, you'll have to adjust to them and speak their languages.

- Being more people-oriented at times will help you reach your goals and win.

"Then one of the scribes came, and having heard them reasoning together, perceiving that He had answered them well, asked Him, "Which is the first commandment of all?"

Jesus answered him, "The first of all the commandments is: 'Hear, O Israel, the Lord our God, the Lord is one. And you shall love the Lord your God with all your heart, with all your soul, with all your mind, and with all your strength.' This is the first commandment" (Mark 12:28–30, NKJV).

As uncomfortable as it may seem, God expects us to love Him using all of these styles. That is the reason Jesus told us the *commandment* to love Him with our heart, soul, mind, and strength. It says "and" not "or," which is a call for all of us to develop our areas of communication that may be weaknesses.

But what about loving others?

And the second, like it, is this: 'You shall love your neighbor as yourself.' There is no other commandment greater than these" (Mark 12:31, NKJV).

It may not be easy to love everyone with our heart, soul, mind, and strength, but we can certainly develop those skills and try. I believe the effort is what counts the most in this commandment. It's loving others like we love our own temperament!

	I	S	C	D
Category	Heart	Soul	Mind	Strength
Pain Points	Feeling disliked	Confrontation	Anything done without excellence	Lack of choices and control
Misperception Points	May be seen as silly	May be seen as a snob	May be seen as uncaring	May be seen as insensitive and rude
Desires	Fun interaction with others	Atmosphere of calm and peace	Clear information and detailed instructions	Results driven. They want to win!
Connection Points	Show interest in them	Lower your tone and slow your pace	Be prepared with facts and data	Be brief. Get straight to the point

A primary I style loves the Lord with their heart.

A primary S style loves the Lord with their soul.

A primary C style loves the Lord with their mind.

A primary D style loves the Lord with their strength.

When a primary I style loves a C with their mind, they're loving their neighbor as themselves.

When a primary C style loves an I with their heart, they're loving their neighbor as themselves.

When a primary S style loves a D with their strength, they're loving their neighbor as themselves.

When a primary D style loves an S with their soul, they're loving their neighbor as themselves.

Connection is not about loving others the way *we* think they should be loved. It's about loving them the way *they* think they should be loved, and ultimately the way Jesus commanded us to love them. I also believe that the more we yield control of our lives to the control of the Holy Spirit in us, the more He empowers us to love others like Jesus does.

Which primary style is Jesus? Of course—He's ALL of them. And He responded perfectly to each style in the way they needed it the most, at the perfect moment that they needed it. One of the greatest examples of this is the story we opened the book with—the woman caught in adultery.

Okay, we get it—her name wasn't Deborah. The Scripture doesn't give us a name for her, so we took a little bit of artistic license there. No harm intended. Let's go back to where we began:

> Now early in the morning He came again into the temple, and all the people came to Him; and He sat down and taught them. Then the scribes and Pharisees brought to Him a woman caught in adultery. And when they had set her in the midst, they said to Him, "Teacher, this woman was caught in adultery, in the very act. Now Moses, in the law, commanded us that such should be stoned. But what do You say?" This they said, testing Him, that they might have something of which to accuse Him. But Jesus stooped down and wrote on the ground with His finger, as though He did not hear.

> So when they continued asking Him, He raised Himself up and said to them, "He who is without sin among you, let him throw a stone at her first." And again He stooped down and wrote on the ground. Then those who heard it, being convicted by their conscience, went out one by one, beginning with the oldest even to the last. And Jesus was left alone, and the woman standing in the midst. When Jesus had raised Himself up and saw no one but the woman, He said to her, "Woman, where are those accusers of yours? Has no one condemned you?"

> She said, "No one, Lord."

> And Jesus said to her, "Neither do I condemn you; go and sin no more" (John 8:2–11, NKJV).

Did you see it? Did you see how Jesus moved effortlessly through strength, heart, soul, and mind?

> "He who is without sin among you, let him throw a stone at her first."

Pause for a second. There are two types of interpretations of the Bible. There is exegesis—which is telling you what the Bible says in its original context; and there is eisegesis—which is basically telling you what I believe may have happened, but don't know solely by the original text. The following is most *definitely* eisegesis. Let's continue...

Jesus stooped down to write in the sand. I believe He was writing the names of the Pharisees who had slept with that woman. Some scholars theorized that Jesus was writing the secret sins of the Pharisees so they could see it for themselves. Either way, it was a *highly* confrontational thing to do to the leading religious leaders of that day. That is a D type on display. He courageously and confrontationally presented the truth, regardless of who could see or hear it. The Pharisees dropped their stones and left.

Then in verse 10, Jesus addressed the woman and said, *"Woman, where are those accusers of yours? Has no one condemned you?"*

In our day and age, addressing a female as "Woman" would be derogatory, but in the culture of Jesus's day, speaking to her made her an equal. This was Jesus's way of tearing down the social and cultural barriers of that day and reaching out with his heart to her heart. This was an I type on display. Reaching her heart with his.

The woman replied, *"No one, Lord."* See it? Her heart had already connected to Jesus so much that she publicly identified Him as *her* **Lord**!

Then Jesus's S type exerted itself and connected with her soul with complete absolution by saying in verse 11, *"Neither do I condemn you . . ."*

How extraordinary! How freeing! How wonderful! A lifetime of shame, heartache, and abuse was washed away in an instant by the love of Jesus.

But He wasn't done, yet.

The C type buttoned it with His mind. *"Go and sin no more."*

He didn't tell her that it was okay to sin. He told her to stop doing so. But before correction was brought, notice that the **connection** was made. That was the pattern of Jesus in the Bible: meet the need, make the connection, and then reveal Himself and His divine plan.

Are we missing something in our lives when we're known more for correcting than we are for connecting? As my friend, Darryl Rivers, says, have we "ETR'd"? Have we "earned the right" to speak into their life? Until we make a connection, the answer is no, and any attempt to correct without connection is an exercise in futility, frustration, and possibly fury.

We need to follow the pattern of Jesus. We must grow beyond only talking to people the way we think we should and start connecting with them in the way they need.

That is the true meaning of Ephesians 4:29 (NKJV): *"Let no corrupt word proceed out of your mouth, but what is good for necessary edification, that it may impart grace to the hearers."*

For years I thought "corrupt word," or in some translations "unwholesome talk," meant being vulgar, but that's not really what that means. In this context, "corrupt" means that the words coming out of our mouths are not edifying others.

"Edify" comes from the same root word as "edifice," which is a wall that is built up.

It's about edifying (building up!) the hearers. We can only edify the hearers by speaking their language.

Using your own language in a foreign country where it isn't spoken isn't edifying anyone. In many cases, it is only frustrating them or causing them to just ignore you. Using your own temperamental language all the time will have the same effect on the hearers.

Let's thank God for the way He God-Wired each of us! Not just ourselves. Let's learn to connect with each other and to the world.

It will make our organizations more productive. It will make our organizations more fun. It will make our organizations more peaceful. It will make our organizations more efficient and excellent.

But most of all, it will fulfill God's greatest commandments:

1. Love Him with all our heart, soul, mind, and strength.
2. Love our neighbors as ourselves.

Let's love each other. Let's love those who are like us and especially those who aren't like us. Doing so will tell the world that Someone special is living in us and through us, and just maybe . . . they'll want to meet Him too.

> *"A new commandment I give to you, that you love one another; as I have loved you, that you also love one another. By this all will know that you are My disciples, if you have love for one another"* (John 13:34–35, NKJV).

About Ken Hartley

Ken Hartley is an international keynote speaker and has authored (some as a contributor and as a coauthor) ten books, including *Hidden Treasures, Leadership Illusions, Leadership Lessons from My Fathers*, and the Amazon bestseller, *DISCover Your Team's Potential*.

He has several certifications in speaking and leadership and is an Advanced Accredited Human Behavioral Specialist in the DISC model of human behavior. Ken travels extensively, speaking to corporations and organizations about leadership, personal growth, and effective communication.

His presentations combine his skills as a speaker, an illusionist, and a singer. They are often described as entertaining, engaging, and transformational. He and his family reside in Chattanooga, Tennessee.

To book Ken to speak at your next event, visit his site at: www.HartleyLeadership.com

About Chris Rollins

Chris Rollins is the president of Rollins Performance Group, Inc., a company that works with operational and sales leadership teams that are serious about achieving growth. He is also led the project as a contributing author of the bestseller, *DISCover Your Team's Potential*.

Chris is an Executive Master Trainer in the DISC model of human behavior. He uses the DISC model to help others learn to communicate more effectively. He also hosts certification classes for those who want to become certified, and better yet, qualified.

Through his impactful keynote presentations, seminar and workshop sessions, books, online courses, or one-on-one consultation sessions, Chris uses his proprietary 3C Model of Performance as his foundation, in order to help his clients achieve consistent and sustainable growth.

To book Chris to speak at your next event or to train your team, visit his site at: www.RollinsPerformanceGroup.com

49714ae5-8405-42ff-a665-b659c6bd4ee4R02